MW00512725

Vote with POWER!

Vote with POWER!

How Voters Can Influence Our Elected Officials!

MAKE YOUR VOTE COUNT!

DENNIS R. BOWERSOX

LIBERTY HILL PUBLISHING

Liberty Hill Publishing
2301 Lucien Way #415
Maitland, FL 32751
407.339.4217
www.libertyhillpublishing.com

© 2021 by Dennis R. Bowersox

All rights reserved solely by the author. The author guarantees all contents are original and do not infringe upon the legal rights of any other person or work. No part of this book may be reproduced in any form without the permission of the author. The views expressed in this book are not necessarily those of the publisher.

Due to the changing nature of the Internet, if there are any web addresses, links, or URLs included in this manuscript, these may have been altered and may no longer be accessible. The views and opinions shared in this book belong solely to the author and do not necessarily reflect those of the publisher. The publisher therefore disclaims responsibility for the views or opinions expressed within the work.

Paperback ISBN-13: 978-1-6628-2510-1

Dust Jacket ISBN-13: 978-1-6628-2511-8

Ebook ISBN-13: 978-1-6628-2512-5

We the voters must get our representatives to hear us,
answer us, inform us, respect us, and represent us. Or they
must get out!

Dennis R. Bowersox

Table of Contents

Preface

My motivation for writing this book came from my dedication to helping Americans return to the lifestyle I enjoyed during my upbringing. I was a youngster in a medium-size city in the Midwest. Life then was much simpler, safer, and more peaceful than today. I could ride my bicycle anywhere in the city as long as I was back by dinnertime. I felt safe. Our family, from my assessment, was of the lower middleclass. We had all we needed to enjoy life. My mother, for the most part, did not have to work outside our home. Most families today need two or more jobs to survive. My father worked for the same company for thirty-eight years and made a middleclass salary. My father paid off the house mortgage as soon as he could. During most of my youth, we had no debt. Tax and inflation rates stayed at an acceptable level.

We had many families as friends, who would be called nuclear families today. That was the lifestyle back then. We knew our neighbors and cared for each other. There were no drug problems at that time. Our family ate dinner together almost 100 percent of the time. Most families today seldom see each other.

My opportunities seemed unlimited. There were few limitations on anyone's opportunities. You could become whatever you wanted to be. I got a good education in the public schools and went on to graduate from three different universities. At that time, you could go to college and graduate without student debt. It is not that way anymore.

Our nation's core values were the same for most people. People wanted safety, freedom, good-paying job opportunities, and to live peacefully and comfortably.

The adults talked politics but only from a Democratic or Republican non-confrontational viewpoint. Most legislation was passed through cooperation from both parties and by the centrists in Congress. There was no bickering, name-calling, or power grabs. Most people got along with each other, whether in neighborhoods, sports, school, church, at work, or in other places for social meetings. We could afford most of our needed health, eye, and dental care. We did not need government's help or have to go into debt. We had the lifestyle we enjoyed.

We spent a lot of quality time with our family and friends. We seemed to have plenty of time for fun, playing games and relaxing together. I frequently visited three or four small businesses in our neighborhood, all of which seemed to be doing well. There were no burned-out buildings in my simple neighborhood.

Often, neighborhood kids occupied their time in sports activities. We had safe parks near us to play in. There was little that a youth needed to worry about or any tough decision to make. I never really appreciated my time growing up until America started changing—not for the better. American history and our culture were important, and we never experienced cancel culture.

Today, there are many problems in America. Because of my fear of the threats and dangers our children and grandchildren face, I needed to speak up. All Americans deserve the lifestyle

I experienced as a child. Our dysfunctional government only adds to our problems.

We the voters can change the systems of our government by getting back our representation. From there, we can build the future that most Americans deserve and want. We can be the solution to America's problems. We can put our divided country back together. There are a few people who will never be happy in America. We cannot keep letting them take us in their direction. Our future generations deserve a safe, peaceful place to live, full of opportunities to develop their potential. We can come together and help all Americans enjoy the country of life, liberty, and the pursuit of happiness. This book and the prescribed road map was created for success is my dedication to uniting voters and changing our dysfunctional political landscape. Please join me by *Voting with Power*.

Chapter 1

Introduction

If you feel our country is heading in the wrong direction, there is something you can do about that. If we the voters don't take action now, we will live in an America we don't like or want.

The purpose of this book is to give all Americans hope for a better future. This can be done through changing the power that the members of Congress have taken away from the voters.

This book is for you if you have any of the following thoughts or feelings or you identify with any of the following statements:

- You are tired of the thick political name-calling, blaming, and bickering.
- You feel our highly paid representatives are not getting anything accomplished.
- You are concerned about the national debt and out-of-control pork spending.
- You are concerned that woke and cancel culture will have devastating effects on our country.

- You want our government to be more efficient and serve the voters like a business does its customers.
- You are concerned about the diminishing number of future opportunities for your family members.
- You are worried about getting criminals off, and keeping them off, our streets.
- You feel your vote does not count.
- You feel our government is out of control.

How did this book come about? Nine years ago, I wrote my second book, *Our Government is Killing Us! An Invitation to Help Fix Our Government and Cure Our Economy.*

Back then I uncovered national problems and wrote about correcting our dysfunctional government. It especially pointed out the areas of the federal government, politics, our government's bad influences on small business, a weak economy, bad financial management, too much government control, and the growing freedom-killing bureaucracies.

I also pointed out the lack of transparency, accountability, and representation. I shared many examples of how our government's out-of-control spending, constant use of pork barrel legislation, and increasing national debt will soon destroy our economy and America.

I did not write that book to make money from book sales. So, I failed at promoting it properly. Therefore, the book sales never gained traction. I gave a few speeches and sold a few books, but my dream was to start a movement of "we the people" who would take action to alter the path our government was on. My dream never came to fruition. This time around it is a must-do plan.

America's problems are more critical to solve than nine years ago. Our government has gotten worse. The symptoms are more pronounced. We see it every day in our representatives' lack of cooperative functioning, constructive behavior, positive language, and judgment. We are not represented due to the ingrained party affiliations and influences. Members of congress act in accordance with what they feel will get them reelected. The problem is they listen to their party instead of listening to their constituents. Plus, now a high percentage of members of Congress are doing nothing of benefit for us. The one thing they are doing that will have a large impact on us and our children is continually adding to our debt. According to the CBO, Congressional Budget Office projections if we stay on the same trend the debt load will be disastrous to our voters economic future. By 2023 the CBO projections indicate the federal debt will reach 107 percent of GDP which is the highest in our history. If the trend continues the federal debt will be 195% of the of America's gross domestic product (GDP). This would mean the Americans national income is only about half of what we, the citizens of the United States of America, owe. High debt will affect citizens by raising taxes, lowering your standard of living, will slow the economy and cause loss of opportunity for your children and grandchildren. Our current administration is attempting to pass over $9 trillion of new spending. We can't pay off our $28.19 trillion debt now. This would, over the next ten years, build our debt to $44 trillion.

The unresolved issues from the past have been magnified. That along with the additional problems are placing America on the threshold of disaster.

A new threat since I wrote my book nine years ago comes from the extensive power of big tech companies. They are a threat to our freedom of speech and choice. Other new dangerous developments come from Antifa, Black Lives Matter, high inner city crime rates, and other destructive behaviors.

There are new forces to deal with since I wrote the last book. A mindset and attitude change is taking over our government and our lives. This new intense power grab comes from members of Congress changing the way they think and respond. Congress' current expression originates out of anger, blame, win at any cost, tough language, and the influence of money. This power grab is constantly observed through our representatives' voices and actions. These attempted power grabs were hidden in past agendas, not today. They are easily observed and out in the open. We are seeing the horrendous power held by a few members of Congress. Those few are running our country.

Our country has major problems. The symptoms are evident. Here are the predominant problems.

1. This past summer's (summer of 2021) big city vandalism, burning buildings, churches, federal buildings, and police stations and destroying businesses. The worst of this is in the number of people hurt, including police officers.
2. The cancel culture movement destroying statues, monuments, and governmental buildings and even books, while attempting to rewrite our past.
3. The tech companies decide who can say what. They are canceling anyone off their platforms who are on the other side of the political divide.
4. The Black Lives Matter movement started with a good cause. The movement soon shifted and became a force of destruction and violent behavior.
5. The lack of progress as members of both parties in Congress no longer cooperate with each other.
6. Two levels of law enforcement systems, creating unequal justice and operating by two standards.

7. The judges who are so liberal they let criminals go free, when the proven recidivism rate should keep them incarcerated. Those who perpetrate heinous crimes and get released too soon often hurt citizens or kill again. A few cities have a no-bail rule. Any suspected criminal goes free.

8. There is too much emphasis on being politically correct. Everyone has their own understanding and belief in what is politically correct. People are overly concerned about being offensive to people placed in groups described by external descriptions as race, gender, culture, or sexual orientation. This hypersensitivity is creating anxiety and confusion of how to refer to people, so no one is offended. This creates unnatural dialogue and worry about how to always be proper. It is confusing and our language is being constantly changed.

9. Our new mode of communication is turning into blaming anyone you do not like, or if you disagree with their political affiliation. That, in today's world, gives you the right and duty to call them racists and bigots openly and quickly.

10. The constant reference to white supremacy, which is getting more pervasive. The definition of white supremacy found in the Merriam-Webster Dictionary is as follows: "the belief that the white race is inherently superior to other races" and that white people have dominance over people of other races. This means that white race in our country is oppressing other races and the other races are being oppressed. The ideology that purports to fix or deactivate white supremacy training has a goal of helping the attitude taking pride in being white and not feeling shame. The white fragility training, which Robin

DiAngelo's book, "white Fragility" focuses on shaming white people for being white and indoctrinates the students in believing that if you are white, you are inherently special and racist. That follows the belief the America is filled with systemic racism. One of the stories in her book was about Jackie Robinson the famous baseball player. Instead of describing the Robinson's success as a tribute to him for breaking the color line, She instruct people to describe him as "Jackie Robinson, the first black man whites allowed to play major league baseball. The ideology has gotten into and is being taught in our military and schools. The teaching, indoctrinates whites in believing that any gain in a black persons growth is not due to their individual work, ability and merit and that myth is to be debunked. This is teaching even our young children that do to being white they are guilty of suppressing people of color. What does this training accomplish for the children's self-confidence and desire to be an American who does not see color? This training was promoted in the framework of critical race theory. It claims to be an attempt at anti-racism training. An article in the *Telegram & Gazette*, referred to a June 25, 202, meeting of the Massachusetts Association of School Committees. The Telegram & Gazette is a daily newspaper located at 100 Front Street Worcester. Massachusetts. The association urged the school district to support a resolution that would offer professional development on diversity, equity, and inclusion for its staff. This training is now being incorporated into the curriculums of many public schools all over our country. The problem is that it is creating more racism as white people are taught to be ashamed about slavery and discrimination even when they had zero experience with this in their lives. The *New York Times* devised "1619 Project," which is, according to the *Telegram & Gazette* being heavily biased and designed to teach students that slavery and racism are at the heart of what the United States of America is and always has been about. Many politicians think we have a nation with systemic race problems. White supremacy training and critical race theory (CRT) will soon cause more racism. Our country has made great gains along racial unity and equality. There is room for a lot more improvement. We need to continuously put in the effort to improve communication, understanding, truthfulness, and justice. Some nationally known minority leaders in our society disagree with white supremacy and feel most of the racist discrimination is being reduced. The white fragility movement purpose is to get white fragility training in all organizations and educational institutions in American. This is causing causing more divisions among our people. This movement is infiltrating our military, schools, and many organizations. The purpose is to get white people feeling guilty for the terrible events that took place in our country's past. They are indoctrinating white people in our institutions to feel ashamed. Their true purpose is trying to advance the position of people of color, especially black people. Instead of building minorities up through education, they are intent on tearing white people down.

11. There have been many uprisings and much destruction caused by Antifa. These are people who hate America. To make their point, whatever that is, they are willing to destroy businesses and the lives of fellow Americans. Where is their conscience?

Many voters are already burned out on our political system. They are taking the easy, short route of giving up. They feel there is no hope. They are wrong. The readers of this book will find a road map and prescribed solutions for our politics and problems. Those who are overly negative and have given up will remain part of the problem. They will not be part of the solution. It will take many Americans working together to alter our situation. The voters with the right attitude and willingness to help by participating in making the changes to our government practices will obtain different, better results for all Americans. We all will enjoy better lives forever. This will improve the lives of all Americans; however, it can only be accomplished with a high percentage of voters taking part.

The thoughts found here are important to you if you want to live in a land of the free, in a safe place, with united citizens, with free speech, no ceiling on your opportunities, a good economy, and mobility. If you want a government that represents the voters, we must change the current system and work to build a better life, liberty, and the pursuit of happiness for all citizens.

This book will give you a new way to get excited about being an American. All Americans, whether Democrat, Republicans, liberal, or conservative, will be enlightened by these fresh ideas. The concepts addressed here will be welcomed by all Americans from all races, religions, creeds, classes, colors, and sexual orientations. This book promotes changing the way Congress functions, the processes, how Congress makes decisions, and who they should be representing: the voters. It was written for the purpose of giving American citizens a better way to communicate with their federal representatives. The content is for anyone who wants to retain what we have left of our culture, our values, history, rights, freedoms, and opportunities. Anyone who wants to live in unity and stop the divide will be interested in reading this.

These pages will inform all those Americans who are frustrated or have fears of the direction we are heading that there is a solution. This is a book for those who do not know what can be done to change our government and solve our many problems. In other words, for all Americans.

You will be provided with the constructs of a new journey and a new organization for getting our congressional representatives to listen to us, inform us, answer us, respect us, and truly represent us, the voters. It is a new system that will hold our representatives accountable and encourage them to be transparent and responsible.

Voters have the great privilege of voting. To add influence on their votes, they have to take on the responsibility of staying involved through providing their input. This book explains how voters can stay engaged in the legislative process. This is the only way for voters to live in the America they want.

The reader will find out how this new development and organizational road map will work and weaken the power the political parties have over us. This movement will lower the influence of the current media and politics over us.

The ideas will, when implemented, help unite us and transcend America from a dysfunctional government into a less political and more productive government. This will be accomplished by uniting all people of America, we will get back on the path of our core values and return to being a country of freedom, safety, unlimited opportunities for prosperity, and the lifestyle most people desire. We need to communicate, cooperate, and have a mission and plan. As we begin using these ideas in a civil manner and start working together, we will see progress. This will improve lives of Americans in a new direction they thought would not be possible. Most Americans are so upset with our government they do not think any approach to change our government exists. When you get burned out and worried, your creativity stops. This journey is not a philosophy but a road map for making successful change. It is for all people who love their American lifestyle. Especially for those who want to protect the best lifestyles for their families' futures, as well as give us improved lives, liberty, and facilitate the pursuit of happiness. In order to maintain and improve our lifestyles we must take action. This includes voter influence and the power to help Congress eradicate our current problems, as mentioned above, and handle challenges in the best interest of all Americans as we work together.

This plan can bring us together, and through it, all voters will share in our progress. We will create mutual understanding through communication. We will learn why we think differently and find a middle ground. From there we can give our information to our representatives so they can pass legislation and run our government in alignment with what the voters advocate.

This journey will make Congress's job easier. Our representatives will first need to accept and adapt to the new processes. This journey and organization will provide a means for the members of Congress to know and understand what their constituents think and want. This will open dialogue within which Congress and the voters can truly see each other's point of view and purpose. The voters will have more input and a better understanding of why their representatives vote the way they do. This means our representatives will represent those who they are supposed to be representing. This new process will lower the representatives' stress level. They currently have a lot of stress from passing bills and laws that are against the will of their own district voters. Currently most of their voting is on behalf of big money influencers or their party, which results in the threat of not getting reelected. How can any representative feel good about their current job performance? They only vote for whatever their party tells them. They will no longer be glued to their party machine. They can perform their jobs as their oath prescribes. They will get higher ratings and recognition and feel good that they are helping America. They will start to vote independently from their party and other influencers. We will see the change as our representatives begin to represent their constituents. This will happen when our elected officials' beliefs, thoughts, engagement, and actions become aligned with the intent of their voters. When functioning in concert with their voters, our representatives will have job security. We the voters won't need term limits.

When our representatives only vote along party lines, they are telling Americans they are against democracy, capitalism, and our constitution, and that they do not care about the lives of their constituents. How do they sleep at night?

We need to move party power back to a centrist position to find common ground. Party power must be eliminated.

Our representatives sign an oath of office. That oath should guide them in keeping focused on serving and representing their constituents. Our current governing atmosphere, processes, and actions have moved a long way away from that oath. We need to remind them and get them back to improving the lives of "we the people." They must stop representing other influences.

We need to stop blaming and yelling at each other. We should all do our part to help people of all races, colors, classes, sexual orientation, and religions. We need to focus on creating an equal path of opportunities and assist all people to reach the lives they want.

Politically entrenched beliefs and actions need to be softened to improve the lives of all citizens. Through this journey, many of our citizens will join us in a united effort to use these plans to improve the lives of all Americans. Our lives will be changed for the better.

We are losing the willingness and ability to trust each other and get along. We need everyone to contribute to our society, be free, and live in a safe community that offers plenty of opportunities. Many people are just giving up. They do not see a path to the high ground.

I have written this book in response to the statements and questions I hear daily. These statements and questions come from family, friends, clients, and the general public. The statements I frequently hear are: "I am frustrated and tired of our government not doing anything of value for us. I am fed up with the politics." The question following the statements is: "Is there anything I can I do about it? Or is it too late? I am just one person with one vote."

This is a road map that lays out a journey for those who are serious about finding what they can do to make the changes we need. It also provides an implementation process, so we get this plan started working and put us on the right track. It explains not only *what* we need to do and *why,* but also *how*.

Our representatives will have a choice. Some representatives will fail to listen to us, inform us, respect us, and represent our beliefs and our way of thinking. They need to stay in tune with the changes we want for our country. We will know where those representatives stand and who they stand with. Those who choose to stay standing with the money influencers will give their voters a choice. The reaction from their constituents, hopefully, will be to be vote those representatives out at their next election. They must go. Those representatives who adapt and begin to work with and for the voters will be rewarded. They will have job security and positive recognition instead of a 15 percent approval rate.

We cannot find common ground without talking in an adult, logical manner and using and promoting common sense. We must eliminate the hidden agendas and work toward understanding all sides of an issue, from all points of view.

Upon reading this book, you will find explanations of our major problems, which are expanding within America. I will explain wokeness, cancel culture, gerrymandering and what effects they are having on us.

From this writing you will get the explanations for why Congress needs to change its approach and use business models to improve our dysfunctional government and how to handle our problems properly and efficiently.

The parties, media, and big money spend all their time dividing us. They use misinformation, lies, disinformation, money, and power to keep us separated, which blocks our willingness to communicate with each other. That divisive, systemic approach, if left alone, will fractionalize, and destroy our country.

This journey and organizational plan will provide safety, opportunities, personal freedom, a great economy, freedom of speech, less bureaucracy, and the ability to live the lifestyle you desire. This change will bring back our natural rights, unalienable rights under the Declaration of Independence.

I think we all want to be free and prosperous. Why don't we work to help all Americans get the same lifestyle and benefits they want? Why is Congress not as concerned about voters' welfare as they are the interests of their party, big money, and big tech?

My purpose is not to persuade anyone to change political parties or to promote any political alliance or agenda. The purpose is the opposite. It is to correct the dysfunctional government and give the power back to the voters. My writing is solely for the purpose of bring us together. We need to move away from politics affecting almost every aspect of our lives. This journey and new organization will be a challenge for all Americans. You can decide to take part, promote unification, help in the development of open, caring communications, and move our country forward. Or you can do nothing and let our government continue to represent the money power factions.

We need to rebuild America for "We the People." We also need to move our country forward and always strive to make it better. Our results will affect the future of all Americans.

We must take back control. We need to be heard, answered, provided honest truthful information, be respected, and represented.

You will find a new model and path to follow for resurrecting the voter values and ideals that our representatives have lost track of. This country's original purpose was to protect and help all Americans. We need honest answers, accurate, timely information, and have our input listened to. We are on level five of importance to our members of Congress. Level five is the worst position to be in as there are four stronger influencers ahead of us. This position gives us little input or influence with our elected representatives. As soon as we vote them into office, we are no longer needed.

If in our representatives' minds, their party comes first. Lobbyists' desires come second. Super Pac's influence comes third. Their big donators, including big tech, come fourth, and we voters follow from there. How do you like being on level five? We can be in first position again.

To regain first position will take the will and persistence of the American voters. This book will show the way. We can, through unity and communication, make the change.

As we travel this journey together, we will regain power and representation. We will have an automatic solution to solve what many voters advocate: term limits. Our journey will remove the need for term limits.

I hope you will read and get some valuable information from this manual. More importantly, I hope you will engage and take action to help the journey and new organization take place. We must all *Vote with Power! Please visit www.votewithpower.com.*

Chapter 2

Where is Our Government Taking Us?

Our representatives are operating in the best interests of their party, themselves, big money, big influence, and big tech. Their focus is not on the voters' wishes. They want us to be silent until their next election.

They are separating voters from any input or power. They are getting stronger and more forceful in the approach to the legislative process.

Members of Congress quickly forget their duty, which is spelled out in the oath they took to represent the citizens of their states. Their constituents. They took an oath to protect their constituents' rights. They also committed to defend and uphold the Constitution of the United States. They are not operating within these duties they signed up for.

Both parties, whichever is in power, develop their own methods of operating to become the ruling class. This is not democracy. This is not what made America the greatest country in the world. If we continue to let political parties rule us, America will never be the same.

Congress is not even taking the basic steps to solve our national problems. Our representatives are content to keep us in the dark and hope we let them be totally in control. They are not leading us in the direction we want to go. They are solving the problems on behalf of their influencers.

Constantly new legislation and executive orders are taking away our free speech, which we are guaranteed in the First Amendment.

The power shift is letting one person in Congress make decisions for all of us. This includes spending decisions, which allocate trillions of dollars or more to whoever they choose to receive it.

Recent news included an interview with one representative from Michigan. Lissa McClain was interviewed on the national television show Fox and Friends on February 15, 2021. The interview can be seen on an article written by Ramone Chiarello of Fox News. The article is Titled "House Representative demands explanation from Nancy Pelosi on extended deployment of National Guard in D.C. The issue is the National Guard has been protecting the Capitol building in Washington, DC, since January 6, 2021. There are no more crowds, no uprisings, no disturbances, threats, or any other reason for Congress to fear for their safety.

The Speaker of the House of Representatives, Nancy Pelosi, has decided to keep our National Guard troops around the Capitol until next fall. We already spent $500 million in the past five weeks from approximately January 16 through February 20 of 2021. What will ongoing National Guard presence at the Capital cost us taxpayers? You can do the math. The Speaker wants us to believe the tax dollars are hers to spend, not ours.

For instance, one of the recent occurrences was our elected Representative from District 10 in Michigan, Lissa McClain, asked Nancy Pelosi for information on the justification and reasons behind keeping the National Guard protecting the capitol building. The alarming news is that Nancy Pelosi did not even respond to the request for information. She as Speaker of the House is supposed to be the leader of all members of the House of Representatives. Not just her party. This indicates the top party leaders are not only keeping we the voters in the dark, but even members of Congress are out of the loop.

This is a destructive road we are on. We are becoming an oligarchic system of government. Those few in power will make all the decisions. It is time we all joined the journey mapped out in this book and either change the way members of Congress represent us or vote them out.

Politicians need our votes, that is how they keep their jobs. Currently, once elected, their interest, paybacks, and votes are all given to the money donors or political parties to meet those entities' expectations. Large sums of money come in from outside their states to help them win their local elections. This money has one purpose: to position politicians and judges to vote the way of the donors. This comes from wealthy people who want to head our country in the direction they choose, not the direction the voters want.

It would take forever to change the current funding laws. Who makes those decisions on campaign funding? The sad answer is the members of Congress. Congress is comfortable and wants the donation money. Because of the pandemic, Congress gave the suffering American people $600. On the same vote they gave billions to foreign countries and other organizations. We need to change the mindsets of our representatives, to put the voters first. If they fail to change their mindset, our option is to get rid of them. We cannot afford to use our money to solve the world's problems. We can be part of the solution, but not the primary bank account. American needs the money to solve our own problems. We cannot saddle our children and grandchildren with heavy debt. When Congress starts working from a sensible budget, there will be extra money for paying down our debt.

This book offers a plan to offset the huge money donations and the ongoing influence bought by big money. Big donations are rewarded by the results of buying our government. It is working for those donors but against the voters.

We voters need to revolt through our right to vote at the ballot boxes. That alone is not enough. Then we need to stay engaged in this new journey to keep our voices heard. We need to make sure we only vote for the candidates who will hear us, answer us, respect us, inform us, and represent us. Wake up, American voters! We can quickly get the attention of Congress with our newly established voter power.

Our representatives need to align their efforts with the voters' needs and desires. Once the voters have the influence back, we will be heard, answered, informed, respected, and represented. Currently, the power of influence is going in the wrong direction and to the wrong people and organizations.

When our elected representatives behave like dictators, they need to be put out to pasture. If this decision-making process can infiltrate our government, either side of the isle, when in power, will continue to make all our decisions and spend all our future income.

It does not matter which party is in power. Behavior like this is way beyond the power given to our representatives. They have crossed a line, and we need to take the power back now. Otherwise, we will lose our control to better our lives through representation.

Take this a step further. If one person in Congress can make the decision to spend billions of dollars, we are in trouble. If both political parties keep operating from a secret agenda, our rights and freedom will eventually be lost forever. We are currently seeing our freedom of speech and freedom to bear arms becoming hot issues. What if the power people in Congress side with one huge company, which they already are, and allow them to crush small competitors? If this continues, we will lose our capitalist system.

Loss of our capitalist system through eliminating competition means you can only buy from one supplier. They set the price, the delivery schedule, and the amount you can buy. They choose who can buy from them. They choose what products you can get; they choose for you. Does that sound like freedom of choice? We are already experiencing the growth of these monopolies. Our government is supposed to protect our freedoms. The government is now protecting the monopolistic giants. This is another major shift.

We need to stop this direction our government is taking us, moving us into socialism. As our government takes over making all our decisions, redistributes the wealth, and destroys our capitalism we will live in a society where production, distribution and exchange are all regulated by our government.

For a great read about our freedoms, get Senator Ted Cruz's book *One Vote Away*. Senator Cruz has in-depth experience with the Supreme Court and their decision-making process. His book explains the truths of what has happened in the past court decisions. He explains how the future of court decisions will be affected by politics and one vote. You need to read his book to get clarity. The book will raise concern for all voters.

Senator Cruz pointed out many facts through actual cases that we the voters must pay attention to. Our free speech is being eliminated by the way Congress is positioning the Supreme Court to become more of a third branch of government. They are attempting to have the Supreme Court modify their interpretation of the laws based on the judges thoughts on changes in society. This is why you frequently hear about the critical appointments made to the Supreme Court by the President of the United States. Attempting to use court packing is a big issue. That is where one party is in power and want the judges to be either conservative or liberal in their views. To court pack means add to the number of judges to offset the number of judges with the opposite conservative vs liberal point of view. The Left wants the role of the court changed to have the ability to alter and judge cases based on how the society has changed, not based on our Constitution. This is not their job or within their authority. The Supreme Court justices are there to interpret the law, not to rewrite the laws.

Congress looks at our Constitution as a set of guiding principles for decision-making. A differing political philosophy is that the purpose of the Supreme Court is to take information from different groups and organizations and interpret them from their political and philosophical points of view. The legality of having an abortion is a good example. This is a highly emotionally charged subject. If the chosen judges on the court at that time had one belief and societal changes indicated that the laws should be interpreted differently from the Constitution, it would be the majority of judges' prerogative to side with their beliefs. This would alter the power and interpretation of our Constitution to match social change. This philosophy renders power to the Supreme Court to modify laws. Senator Cruz wrote, and I paraphrase, that Congress thwarts citizens' political speech while it has a different standard for corporations such as CNN and the *New York Times*.

Senator Cruz went on to write about the Jim Crow case of *NAACP v. Alabama*. The court ruled the state government of Alabama could not make the NAACP hand over their list of donors. The reason was giving donors' names to the state might create undue persecution from the government.

On a different issue, Senator Cruz, in his book, went on say there is a huge discrepancy in which party receives most of the super PACs' donations. He stated that in the 2016 elections the super PACs donated a total of $611 million toward election campaigns. With the previous discussed court hearing super PAC'S can donate as much and to whom they wish without needing to name doners. This is a discrepancy in our election fairness.

One party got 69 percent of that money. Do you think those donations were trying to buy privileges and benefits in the future?

He went on to explain how one particular party is constantly attempting to get rid of the First Amendment. If they did so, we would lose the protection for all Americans' free speech.

Senator Cruz provided some insight I had not thought about. The true essence of Article One was to protect free speech under the rule of law. Article one is aimed at what he wrote and is considered "unreasonable speech." This means that not only normal speech is protected, but speech that is unusual and disturbing to some is also protected. If everyone agreed that we use accepted speech, Article One would not be needed.

He went on to say that the First Amendment protects us from our government deciding whether what we say is reasonable or not. Does this sound like Big Brother?

Senator Cruz made this statement that when our elected officials, the members of our federal house of representatives and members of the senate, take the oath of office, it is not as a member of the Democratic or Republican party. The representatives' duty is to represent the citizens of their state, to fight for the rights of all citizens, and to defend and uphold our United States Constitution. This source was found in history.house.gov under oath of office. We need to remind all our representatives of their oath and what it means.

On January 10, 2021, according to *Business Insider,* "the editor of Forbes Magazine urged companies not to hire communications staff from the Trump Administration, Sean Spicer, Kayleigh McEnany or Stephanie Grisham." *The Hill,* on January 31, 2021, published an article claiming top level officials are having a tough time getting accepted in new jobs. An article written by Daniella Byck on November 10, 2020, in the news and politics section of the *Washingtonian,* said there was a new organization called Trump Accountability Project whose stated purpose was to hinder Trump staffers from getting private sector jobs, just because they worked for the opposite political party. This is disgraceful. According to an article written on January 21, 2021, in "The Hill" by Alex Gangitano, Corporate American is showing no signs of rushing to snatch up the vast majority of high – level Trump officials. He went on to say that near the end of 2020 was a tough job finding time. But U. S. companies have further distance themselves from Republicans following the deadly mob attack on the Capitol which took place earlier in January 2021.

Harvard students signed a petition to take degrees earned at Harvard away from those who worked in the last federal government administration. They are trying to cancel our freedoms and our futures. Should we cancel all college degrees of those who do not like our political views? We are now experiencing people being fired from jobs because they have political views that differ from those of their employer. Many causes for the firings take place out of work. The employee on their own time posted something on social media that showed political preference that the company did not like. Where does this stop?

From this, I now understand what gives us true free speech and allows dialogue in which smart minds can discuss and educate each other to understand the other person's point of view, which we need to fight to retain our rights of free speech.

Members of Congress represent their state citizens first. But they get paid from tax dollars from all taxpayers from every corner of the United States. They need to represent all citizens. Their oath also includes requiring their efforts to defend the Constitution. My question to you is: are they functioning within their oath of office or are they representing other factions? Some are in violation of our Constitution.

We hire them with our votes. We pay them with our tax dollars. How can they work for someone else? This must change so that they represent the voters once again.

Often our representatives are not open with us to explain their proposals based on the merits they see as value to the voters. They just want us to stop asking for details and justification for how they voted. How transparent or accountable is that?

Congress operates under the influence of those who helped them get elected and vote based on their big money donors opinions, assumptions, assumptions, and judgements. They do not consider what is best for their voters and America. How often do your representatives want your opinion and insights? When was the last time they called you, wrote to you, sent you a questionnaire or a survey, or added you to a focus group? The answer for most of us is never! Unless it is in the middle of an election year for them.

Many representatives, particularly from one party, are attempting to take us into what they call democratic socialism.

The significant belief of the democratic socialists, those on the far left, is to do everything for us, including thinking for us. They feel their mission is to take care of us, as that is one of their core values. They believe in groupthink. Wikipedia defines groupthink as "a psychological phenomenon that occurs within a group of people in which the desire for harmony or conformity in the group results in an irrational or dysfunctional decision-making outcome." This definition can be found at en.m.wikipedia.org. This includes only those who think like they do. They believe we need their protection and help. Their arrogance shows up when they want us to do what they say. They want voters to sit down and be quiet.

Examples of groupthink through our history were written in a *Psychology Today* article, titled Group Think, November 1971, by Irving Janis and other articles can be found in other online sources. (pychologytoday.com.) Often referred to groupthink examples include The Bay of Pigs, the bombing of Pearl Harbor, the collapse of Swissari, and the mass resignation of Major League Umpires Association. For more, Google groupthink.

This year has been full of examples of our elected officials setting rules for the citizens. They violate their own rules. As they have broken those same rules, they have been caught. They feel they know what is best for us. They believe they are better than us. therefore, they are above the rules they hold us to, which means they make judgment calls on our behalf because they "know what we need and want." They go forward without finding out what we really need and want. Another political shift is they forgot they work for us.

If our representatives can become Big Brother, it will cause us, as individuals, to become weak, dependent, lose our sense of self-worth, freedom, hope for a better life, and pride in our own accomplishments.

We will end up a nation of dependent people who lack initiative, creativity, and self-respect. If we allow Congress to impose their will on us, we will become sheep. Is that what anyone really wants?

We have the best nation for individual opportunities, motivation, inspiration, ingenuity, and a passion for self-worth. We need to keep our willingness to help others live in freedom with opportunity, to stabilize and grow our confidence by controlling our lives and lifestyles for ourselves. The groupthink mentality is not what we need, want, or should vote for. How can Congress do their job of representing the voters without any voter input?

My intent is to clarify and ask you, the reader, to gain a clear perspective and understand how our government runs differently than a successful business. Some of government's approaches are not exactly the same as businesses' and rightfully so. However, many of the issues, processes, and legislation should be run like a business.

To make my point, I have included in this book ideas of how, if you owned a business, you would see, think, and act differently from the way Congress operates. My purpose for suggesting this approach is to get every one of our representatives to have a working knowledge of business. Plus, many of you, the readers, own a business or are thinking about starting one. We together will discover why and how Congress should use this information. This book will point out why utilizing a successful business model would greatly improve our government processes.

Many people will disagree with me in how important business skills and knowledge are to running our government. If that represents your thoughts, please read further with an open mind. Congress makes decisions and votes through a small and short-term vision. They only see the trees and are missing the forest. They also vote to support today's goals and situation and fail to look into the future.

When you compare elements of our government to a business, there are and should be similarities to a successful business. We have income and expenses, debt, branding issues, systems and processes, culture, teams, hiring, screening, and onboarding new people, leadership styles, team building, financial management, and operational systems.

In what areas should our government emulate a successful business? Our government processes lack setting goals, they do not operate with defined purposes, they do not create plans, they do not design metrics for result tracking, and they lack good communication systems. Legislation according to en.m.wikipedia.org has many purposes: to regulate, to authorize, to outlaw, to provide funds, to sanction, to grant, to declare or to restrict. Since laws and bills before they are passed are frequently discussed and modified many times. The process itself is not conducive for business type goals. The goal setting, I am referring to is the use of SMART goals. If goals are not **specific, measurable, attainable, reasonable,** and **timely**, they are not goals, but hopes. With my business clients I always introduce my Seven Ps to make sure their activities will get the results they want. The seven Ps are **purpose, plan, practice, persistence, processes,** and **perfect.** Look at any legislation. Does it follow and incorporate the seven Ps? Congress fails in having duties and task descriptions showing how our representatives (employees) listen to us, answer us, inform us, respect us, and represent us.

I point this out because our representatives must have knowledge and skills in leading and making decisions, gained from having an administrative job. They also need experience and skills in running an organization or business. We are heading for a further shift into an oligarchical government. Therefore, our current representatives do not want to operate as a business.

If we looked at our representatives' backgrounds, how many of those in office have experience and success in managing or running a successful business or organization? Congress is taking us on a path of decisions and changes that are not made based on a mission, goals, or plans, or using implementation systems, defined responsibility, or tracking methods. There is no operational system in place except for the laws that establish some processes. Our country is just reacting to issues. There is no planning. Our representatives are driving our car using the rear-view mirror. Without business sense they miss the big picture and the need to research the effects of their decisions and clarify how the changes will affect our futures. They are just trying to solve problems; they do not work on improving America.

For instance, if you managed your business mostly from the wishes and opinions of outside influences, your business would be in trouble. I have coached businesses that have a high percentage of sales from one or two customers. This is extremely dangerous. Yet Congress has a few huge donors, whose influence undoubtedly affects its decision-making process. Members of Congress seldom listen to the important people, the voters; therefore, they fail at promoting good morale, good service, or pass legislation that is in the best interest of all American citizens.

Our representatives have little responsibility for which we hold them accountable. We do not have a process or system in place that evaluates what they do in relationship to what they are supposed to do, which is representing us, the voters. Their authority to control is way out of balance with their responsibility and their job calling. The representative actions and votes are not in line with any agreed-on responsibility. Once they pass legislation, in their minds their responsibility ends.

If you made bad decisions in your business, could you just forget about those decisions? The answer is no. Your decisions produce good or bad impacts, which you have to live with. Your employees, vendors, and customers suffer from any bad decisions you make. They would directly or indirectly hold you responsible.

By holding our representatives accountable, they would have to pay more attention to us, our wishes, and the results that affect us. Later in this book I will explain how we can make the change to hold them accountable through transparency and performance reviews.

Our current nonaccountable, irresponsible, nontransparent government is leading us in a dangerous direction. Most Americans feel we cannot trust our representatives. When our elected representatives do not communicate with us, we can only assume they have hidden agendas. Therefore, they act with seemingly sneaky behavior. This behavior does not pass the smell test. It fails to build unity or trust.

Many years ago, when I was a psychology teacher and counselor, I loved the students. But there was one behavior that always upset me. I did not like the behavior of the few students who were not truthful and operated in a sneaky manner. Without trust, it is difficult to have safe and open communication. This hinders any relationship or organization from providing a positive atmosphere in which to move the business, organization, or government in a positive, caring direction.

Years later when I started my real estate investing business, I once again came across a few tenants who were sneaky and lied to me. That behavior was still unacceptable. You can love the people but not accept their behavior. We have a few members of Congress who hide their agendas from us. This represents sneakiness and is unacceptable. We need to eliminate that sneaky behavior or eliminate those who possess it.

Do you think members of Congress are truly proud of what they have accomplished for their voters? One can only gain true job pride by delivering the outcomes that the job requires. Our current governmental legislative process fails to have our representatives deliver the voters' desired outcomes. The current system fails to measure how our representatives' efforts and actions align with the voters' wishes.

Financial management is a good example of government failures. This is a critical way our government is taking us on a dangerous path. In your business, if the leadership overspend the budget by millions of dollars, what will happen?

Most of the legislation being passed is voted for by our representatives pressuring each other to give in. The way to get votes is to trade huge amounts of money for any purpose a representative wants, usually unrelated to the issue at hand. This is a systemic problem and a recurring process. This will continue to be the way to get votes, in order to pass legislation, unless we stop it. It also sets up a bad atmosphere, of "I did you a favor financially; now you owe me a financial favor."

It is not based on explaining the merits of the bill, which should be the only reason Congress votes for or against every bill. If you must trade millions of dollars to get your bill passed, it should not be passed. If the bill needs financial rewards not related to the bill to get it passed, this shows the purpose of the bill is not worthy of getting votes.

Our members of Congress misinterpret and misuse the Constitution to get more power. They are taking on a higher level of authority than they should have, especially when they have a low level of responsibility.

In your business, if you have positions with authority and responsibility that are out of balance with each other, you have frustrated employees and employees creating major problems.

You need to balance their job responsibility with their job authority. This would allow for everyone to have a safe environment and be on the same business mission. By everyone doing their job, they would improve productivity and efficiency and create a team with high morale and a culture and atmosphere conducive to working together.

Congress manipulates their authority and responsibility to get their way, not the way of the voters.

According to the way our members of Congress are acting, most do not honestly care about their constituents, except for their votes. When it comes to our families' financial futures, they constantly outspend the budget. Many times, our government has no adherence to a n operating budget, has people in the wrong seats, and fails to have an operational plan. Their focus on the voters comes about when they need votes to keep their jobs in the next election.

The direction our representatives are taking us can be understood by asking some questions. To have transparency, voters need to ask: How do people get elected to Congress and come out being multimillionaires while working for us?

Our new journey will make this situation transparent, as we take over the running of our country's business through repositioning our power and getting our representatives to use our input.

Currently we have representatives who do not understand or have skills in finance or business management, while others in Congress do have the knowledge but do not care about our counties financial future. They just get away with abusing it.

What would you do if your financial managers took your retirement funds and spent them? Besides removing those who took the funds, the main concern would be how to rebuild that fund. Do you ever hear any representative talking about finding ways to rebuild our Social Security funding? The answer to that question is no. Our representatives are financially shortsighted. Plus, in their minds, "It's not my problem." They are too busy spending billions of dollars with zero results in the best interests of America. Congress just keeps kicking the underfunded Social Security program down the road.

I once had a manager for one of my businesses who ran out of money is his checkbook. He kept writing checks until the bank closed the account. You are out of business when you start writing bogus checks. Our government is writing bogus checks every day.

Our elected representatives are not punished, are not held accountable, never pay it back, or get fired, except when they lose a reelection. They just keep getting reelected and getting their spending privileges back.

What should we do with the Congress that took our Social Security money and spent it? When are they going to pay it back? The answer is never. Hopefully, a program will be put into place to fund the Social Security program before it is no longer available to the rightful owners of those funds. It is the taxpayers' money. The American people are told Social Security is an "entitlement." You have got to be kidding! The truth is that to our representatives, financial mismanagement is a "so what?" problem.

This new business approach and journey will put pressure on Congress and make them recognize that they need to manage our tax dollars responsibly. They need our attention and guidance. Without those they will not change.

The question is: How do we get their attention? Get them listening to us, answer us, inform us, respect us, and get them to represent us. We need to show them we are taking back the power and their job security is on the line.

This book offers an approach and opportunity that I have created. I have been looking for ideas and support from anyone who identifies with my concerns and has any kind of solution. All I find is frustration and no ideas offered for resolving our government process. We have allowed our government to take us on a wild ride away from where we need to be. If this new journey is of interest to you, please keep reading. Most voters feel left out, frustrated, and out of the loop. This manual offers a way to change your thinking, if you are fed up with overbearing dense politics, wasteful spending, having no voice, and Congress abusing your children's money.

Now is the time for voters to claim our rights by getting members of Congress to hear us, answer us, inform us, respect us, and represent us. They need business processes and operational systems to turn this country around.

Chapter 3

Our Government Is Attempting to Change Our Core Values

Who are we? Who do we want to be?

During this chapter I will share examples of where our government is trying to change or take away some of our core values.

For the sake of understanding, I use the practical definition of values as being issues in your life that are right and important. If it is a core value, both what is right and what is important need to be connected.

The American people have core values, which our government has a duty to protect. We want and deserve our right to have Congress working for us and representing the voters. Our government's attempt to change our core values is crucial to our elected officials. The value change they want is to stop representing us and move to a level of controlling us.

One of the social core values is to live under the Golden Rule. Do unto others as you would have them do unto you. The new government Golden Rule is not what we want. It is do unto others who do not believe, think, or speak like you. A political party's goal is to silence us, cause damage to our culture, get in our faces with politics, and cancel us. For those representatives who don't want this format, they are too afraid or too deep in alliance with their party to do anything about it. How does this new core value of what is right and important fit unity and progress for all?

We all have sets of values such as personal, family, business, organizational, health, educational, and group. Our individual values, those we live within, are the beacons of our behavior. We rely on our values as our moral compass. A partial list includes honesty, safety, equality for all, being treated fairly, having, and sharing opportunities for success and prosperity, truthfulness, pride in our nation, importance of family, freedom, liberty, and justice for all.

These represent what we believe in, and think is just for ourselves and others. We need to focus on what in our lives is right and important.

The goal has changed for politicians. Politicians' mission has become winning their next election and controlling through power, in addition to supporting and voting along their party lines. It is no longer to service the best interests of our people. Our elected officials' approach has changed to being more radical, outspoken, and argumentative to sell their message. This alters our lives as we are losing the important core values we want, one of them being civility.

Instead of valuing living in harmony, politicians are promoting disruption and even violence in our lives, because of the inability of Congress to solve our problems.

Our forefathers' core values were, and still should be followed, to provide American citizens with life, liberty, and the pursuit of happiness. Those are our unalienable rights.

Our core values are built into our culture. Our culture is based on our core values. Our politicians, big money and media have taken away the voter core values of the past. They are changing our culture. We stand for truth, caring for others, the safety of others, the common ground of dialogue, supporting each other's opportunities and creative freedom, having pride in our country, family, and self, being model citizens, and being rewarded by peace of mind and having unlimited opportunities.

Concern for our individual and all Americans' safety is another area where some members of Congress and the judicial system are failing us. We have street rioting, businesses being destroyed, police being abused and killed, and ordinary citizens getting hurt and even being killed. Our government, in many parts of our country, just turn their heads. A core value we all need if we want to survive and be safe is to condemn crime, separate the criminal elements from our society, and provide equal justice.

Today it seems as if the criminals are the victims. It is a fact that if criminal activities are allowed to continue, they will grow and get worse. We need to tell our representatives that crime must be stopped now. Otherwise, it will be in your back yard soon. If it isn't already.

A core value that most Americans want is honesty. We have fallen into the hole of half-truths, lies, and using semantics to bend the truth. People eating at an outside restaurant are being abused or have people in their faces yelling at them. Instead of telling us the whole truth, the media and some legislators are not being honest with us. They tell us this behavior is not mob insurrection, it is just a peaceful protest. You get to decide if Congress and the media are honest with us. This weakens our trust, which our culture relies on for our comfort and security.

Politicians' destructive core value approach is to build mistrust of the other party. They blame, bash, complain, and push their agenda, operating from opinions and personal judgment, not making decisions based on facts, and having a positive purpose.

If you listen to our politicians, they are all about themselves, their power, their party, and their influences. They spend most of their time complaining about a person from the other party or, even worse, about those who are affiliated with the other party.

We should ask our representatives what they have accomplished in the last year on our behalf. Do they have any positive practical ideas about how to add value to America and our lives?

If you owned a business, would your employees be worth $174,000 a year salary while failing to do their job? If you had employees who had zero positive effect on your business and were just living the lifestyle of a "poor me" complainer, what would you do? A core value of most American workers is to be productive in doing their job. They care and have pride.

Most people do not like trash-talkers or negative, aggressive people in their lives. Why should we as voters permit these representatives' behaviors to go on?

The value of having our representatives focus on the best interest of "we the people" has changed. Respect for citizens has been overruled by the priority of getting power, money, and control. The voters need to turn around our representatives to give us the facts, the truth, the whole truth, and nothing but the truth. How many times, except for election time, have you ever gotten the total information on what is in a proposed bill and then was asked your opinion and thoughts?

Congress's core values have changed. They want to keep us in the dark, not tell us the whole truth, and restrict our freedom to stay involved. It is the country of the people, not a country for just 535 members of Congress.

How do you represent someone when you do not communicate with them?

The parties no longer see or believe they have anything in common with each other. How does this fit with our value of being able to live in peace? The party politicians no longer get along, care about unity, or willingly work together. If the employees in your business had these attitudes, destructive behaviors, and unwillingness to work together, what would you have to do? The only answer is to get rid of the employees who exhibit these negative attitudes. If our representatives in Congress are not willing to change to our specification, they must go.

Why do we vote for and continue to vote for employees, our members of Congress, who are non- productive and worse being destructive, if we would never hire or retain them in our businesses?

Let us change our approach to make better voting decisions. We need to make sure candidates have goals, ideas, and plans to move our country forward. This includes both new candidates and incumbents. We must stop voting for those with the most money backing them for advertising, those who are best at abusing the image of their competitor, and those who are good at selling us false hope. We need to stop voting 100 percent along party lines. We can no longer accept our elected leaders who only see blue or red.

The politicians we need to vote for are those who have positive, workable agendas, the right attitude, and the experience we need. They must understand and care about financial management and are willing to be held accountable for giving us measurable, expected results.

We need to find out if they fit our caring, communicating, positive team approach to helping others. We need to make sure they fit our core values and culture.

Many members of both parties need to grow up, answer our questions, respond to our input, and represent us.

When representatives only run-on conflict and hate, they will no longer be acceptable as our representatives. Most representatives never seem to have any positive thoughts, plans, or ideas to help the American people. Why do we keep them in Congress?

In the last four years we have experienced what I consider to be the worst social climate ever in America. One that should be embarrassing to our representatives and all Americans. This type of behavior must stop. We have representatives in Congress and past directors of the FBI and CIA who are dishonest, liars, unethical, and without integrity. This should be upsetting to our citizens because these people lack the qualities to be our leaders. More importantly, we do not want our children to identity with and imitate these behaviors.

Some individuals on national media outlets stated that the president of the United States was a Russian spy and was colluding with foreign powers. This was factually proven false through three years and $44 million. One of the alarming conclusions is that the individuals making those statements are corrupt, immoral, dishonest liars. This cannot be accepted no matter what party attempts to do it again. We have a core value of justice for all. To have equal justice, we need to enforce our laws. By not enforcing them, we are not providing justice to the citizens who are living within the laws.

How they sleep at night and why we put up with these types of people, I will never understand.

If you had a neighbor who frequently came to your home and was a liar, dishonest, and without any respect to members of your family, would you want them around your children and grandchildren? *I hope your answer is* No. You would send them home.

We need to send some members of Congress home from either side of the aisle: those who are supposed to be leaders and are not, those who fail to act in a professional manner, and those who fail to diligently work on improving our lives or representing us.

We elect representatives, and when they are in office, we need to watch for those who do not represent us and those who stray from our moral compass. We want our children to learn to follow the right moral compass, which will guide them through life. We want our children to follow the words and behaviors of the leaders we respect, not those who embarrass us.

Our country's strength of economy and unparalleled opportunities for all are examples of how great a society can be. This will not last if we do not cull the politicians who only are interested in getting reelected, creating chaos and disruption, and do not help advance our economic system and unlimited opportunities.

In the right business model, you need to keep in touch and engage with your customers. In our current government model, after the election, the voters lose engagement with, attention from, and influence over the candidates. There is no consistent continuing two-way communication. Read the journey section of this book, and you will find a way to take part and make the needed changes.

The power and direction of each representative's vote is often used as a reward for the person or group who supplied the money and has the influence. Not who voted for that candidate. Big money individuals, big business, big banks, lobbyists, and big tech companies take over the influence the day after our elections take place. They get their issues brought to the front, they get their wishes granted in votes and legislation, they get the pork and benefits of legislation that is in their favor.

We the American people are only important to our representatives until we vote. The next day we lose our representation, any transparency, attention, influence, and our ability to hold our representatives responsible, transparent, and accountable.

In the right business model, you use open, honest discussion for the purpose of educating all involved. You understand who the stakeholders are and make sure their voices are heard and they are represented. In our government the model is to argue, blame the other side, and use every bit of your power to win. Our representatives need to learn that the purpose in arguing is to win. The purpose for discussing is to educate and understand each other.

With the constant arguing there is no willingness to see other points of view. There is no growth, no common ground, no cooperation, and no progress made on behalf of the American people.

One of our critical core values is living in a society that provides equal justice. Even that value is being attacked. Some politicians want to change the founders' purpose behind creating the United States Supreme Court. This was referenced earlier but also fits here as a core value. Instead of the original purpose, which was to litigate conflicts in reference to our Constitution and to check that the legislation and the behaviors relating to those legislative rules are in alignment with the Constitution of the United States of America, some politicians want to alter the purpose of the United States Supreme Court to become another means to change laws. This is in violation of its true purpose. It is evident that our Supreme Court has become politically influenced. Which cases they take and how they individually vote seems to be slanted on their political beliefs.

I hope through reading this book you will become more passionate and in alignment with us getting on this prescribed journey with the road map to our future. By having Congress hear us, answer us, inform us, respect us, and represent us, we will *Vote with Power*.

Here is a core value checkup. Please circle the personal core values you believe your representatives should have. Next, highlight the core values you feel they have. See the gaps?

Next, rate each of the core values you desire Congress to have and use a 1–10 scale. This will indicate which values are important to you and how they align with the thoughts and behaviors of your representatives.

Adaptable, Diligent, Joyful, Respectful
Appreciative, Discerning, Kind, Responsible
Attentive, Discreet, Able to Lead, Defender of citizen safety.
Available, Efficient, Loving, Secure
Careful, Equitable, Loyal, Self-Controlling
Committed, Fair, Meek, Sincere
Faithful, Merciful, Submissive
Compassionate, Fearless, Observant, Tactful
Concerned, Flexible, Optimistic, Team member
Confident, Forgiving, Patient, Temperate
Considerate, Friendly, Peaceful, Thorough
Consistent, Frugal, Persevering, Thrifty
Contented, Generous, Persistent, Trustworthy
Creative, Grateful, Prudent, Truthful
Decisive, Honest, Punctual, Uncomplaining
Deferent, Humble, Purposeful, Understanding
Dependable, Reliable, Virtuous
Determined, Possessing Integrity, Resourceful

After you complete this two-step process, there is a question that needs to be answered. Are we electing the right representatives, the ones who share our core values?

Here is one critical core value that is being tested. Do you a want powerful federal government with all the power over the states and your freedoms? Or do you want states to be mostly independent, which means the states oversee their own voting regulations, laws, and law enforcement? There are some issues that we need our federal government to have the power over, such as interstate commerce, federal taxes, national defense, and safety from terrorists, as well as other issues of national concern.

There are many people who believe in both sides of this issue. If you go back and study our history, you will find that our forefathers wanted most of the power left with the states as opposed to the federal government. One advantage the states have is they can compete against other states. This is becoming more relevant is attracting more citizens. This is expressed by the numbers of people moving out of some states and into a few others. This is a gain for the state expanding its population. People don't want to be treated as one homogenous group. We want our independence. Different states offer different cultures, opportunities, levels of safety and freedom. The federal government seems to want to put all cultures, income levels, and lifestyles under one umbrella. Federal laws are passed as if one size fits all. This is not the way our country can be managed. Different regions and states and even areas within each state are different in many ways. How can a federal government minimum wage work in all areas of our country? It cannot!

We now have different states and large cities enforcing their laws in different ways. Some states and local municipalities manage their laws in liberal or conservative manners. This is creating divisions. When individuals choose to move to a different state, it may be due to issues of safety, justice, opportunities, jobs, and other reasons. Some states are lax on law enforcement, weak on locking up criminals and enforcing fair and just incarceration. People who oppose this weak law enforcement fear for their safety. They can and are moving to a different state.

In the past, people moved to another state primarily to get a job, because of the weather, and for health reasons. This is all changing due to the opposing approaches of our federal and state governments.

This will become a state-by-state competitive advantage in gaining population. Those states that align their values and laws with the people they want to attract will be the population growth winners.

If you do not like the rules of one state, if you disagree with your state laws, level of justice, voting rules, or population mix, you have options. Many people are also tired of their state's political entrenchments and prejudices. You have the freedom, if you can afford it, to move to another state. Decisions regarding preferred lifestyle and culture are creating a great division between states. This will change our demographics.

This trend of citizens moving is enhanced by working remotely; lots of people have options of where they want to live. How many Americans will move away from crime, crushing business laws, hyperpolitical control, and hypocrisy?

We need to define and strengthen our core values with our representatives. We need to rebuild our culture, so it benefits all Americans. To do this we must *Vote with Power*.

Chapter 4

How the Media is Dividing Us.

The media outlets in our country have evolved away from being newscasters to becoming influencers.

They want our attention to have job security and give us their slanted opinions and judgments. They want to position us to follow their agenda. They have become promoters of propaganda and purpose-driven organizations.

When is the last news article you read or heard that offered any ideas on how to make America a better country? There are only a few, if any, news articles or programs giving ways to help improve the lives, liberty, and freedoms of us the American people. The media is too busy writing their negative slants on why we should stay divided. They need to be called out for this and for being disruptors.

True journalism in this country is about gone. In the past, journalist presented facts, the law, and non-prejudiced information from all those involved. Journalism, years ago, moved away from the truth and facts. Books have been written for years about the media bias. For example, In his book, Bias, Bernard

Goldberg wrote how the media is distorting the news. He was a CBS news journalist and knew what was happening from an insider's experience. In his book he explains how the bias has created a hidden agenda. Today's news outlets slant the information by who they interview, what pictures they show us, and the dialogue as if it were the whole truth. This is selective information to support their views. They have moved further away from the real news. Now they have boxed us in with their opinions and judgments. We have experienced the shift from journalism to a different purpose. Writers now want us to listen to their beliefs and follow their judgements. Even worse, they have become influencers to get us to believe their position is the right one. Today's level of media corruptions is taking place as the media is molding us to believe, think, and act and vote as they do.. This gives them control over the audience.

We need to show the media we want the truth; we are their job security, and we count. We are smart, we want freedom of thought, speech, and our independence. If we do not stop accepting what they feed us, they will continue to deliver their opinions and manipulate us. When the journey explained through this book is implemented and the media sees the number of our members and our impact, they will be forced to change or die out.

Our journey will be a true test of how the lifestyles most citizens desire are similar. We are not so different from each other. We are more like a bell-shaped curve, and there are a small percentage of voters on either the far left or far right.

The media, Big Tech, and Congress want to keep us separated in thought, so they keep us from communicating with each other. The media only shows us the side they want, often in favor of one political party. They are splitting our political powers and representatives along their belief lines. They provide selected and prejudiced information.

We need to unite and move the power away from Congress and the media. Both members of Congress and the media will find out how badly voters want to keep their independence of thought. The media and politicians act as if we are all far left or far right. My assumption is that when we look at our core values, we will find that most of Americans share the same ones. As stated in the last chapter, those personal core values are defined by what is right and important. We are not that different in the lifestyles we all want.

To understand and enjoy those common ground lifestyles, we need to come together. This will be done through building communication systems, sharing information, being considerate in our opinions and judgments, and working together. We need to strive to improve the lives of all Americans.

The media is slanted to present current events from their opinions, judgments, and their political philosophies. We are prodded to see their side of the issue and not the whole picture or all the facts. They think it is important to direct us to the news they want us to know about and see. Their purpose, besides selling their information, is to keep us separated. Separation advances the power in their beliefs and keeps us vulnerable to wanting and believing in their information. We must first all agree that most media outlets are divisive and cause Americans to argue and dislike each other's behaviors.

It is spilling over from disliking the opinions of others to disliking those who have those opinions. The media covers news from their own viewpoint. Black Lives Matter, Antifa gatherings, and cancel culture outbursts are exposed by some media while covered up by others. This is a huge negative aspect of our nation. We have always had a slight disliking for other political beliefs that were different from ours. But the historic slight dislike has evolved into deep hate. Most of the media have become cheerleaders for stirring up more hate.

We have been led too far; we live in hate for the sake of political correctness, which is based on everyone's individual point of view. Politics needs to take a back seat to the more important issues of how we live our lives and how we can get along and care about each other. The media does not want us voters to think for ourselves or be independent in using our brain power. They are causing the voters to argue instead of finding common ground. They sell us the disaster and conflict and urge us to feel good about demeaning the other side of the aisle so they can sell more information. Some of our government leaders have jumped across the ethical and probable legal line by sharing confidential information with the media. The media then exposes this information to the public before researching its accuracy.

The media wants to keep all our attention focused on politics and the bad elements of people in our country. Not the criminals but the people who do not agree with us.

If you watch CNN and then Fox News, you will get totally different presentations. The problem is that most Americans who still watch the news tend to always watch the same channel. So, they are getting only part of the events from the viewpoint of that station. Some stations are giving slanted opinions instead of what really happened and is happening, not just in the words they use, but the people they select to interview and the pictures they choose for their audience to see.

Check it out for yourself. Choose one event that just took place and see the difference on both channels. You will not believe they are reporting on the same event. The media controls what they want you to see and hear. Often, they report on some events and ignore others, as if those events never occurred.

From one source you may not even know a situation happened. No matter how important or unimportant, the American public wants true and unbiased information. The journey I am prescribing will give you the truth, the whole truth, and nothing but the truth. Then get your opinions and share them with your representatives.

We need to use individual intelligence and objective thought processes, not what the media wants us to believe. The good news is we do not need the nationally recognized media to get accurate government information. There are podcast, radio programs and internet to get accurate information. You of course have to be diligent in checking out the source. Once we are on our new journey, we will share our opinions and stay away from following the pushing, agendas, and prejudices of the media. We will remain an integral part of what is happening in America. This reform will resurrect our privilege of staying involved. This will give us great pride in helping design and guide our country's future. We will return to a government of the people, by the people, and for the people. This will head us back in the direction of sharing domestic tranquility, which we are losing!

We need to unite, stay calm, be flexible, and drive our country in the direction we, the voters, want. Stop being stirred up by the media's disruptive agenda and false views.

The media strives to dominate the message of how our country is doing and where it should be heading. The news outlets use demonization and accusations to convince us that people who disagree with their viewpoint are bad people. We need to build unity and stop listening to a media that promotes a divided country. They spend much of their news time bashing the view and even the personalities of those who differ with their political stance.

A February 8, 2021, article by Joe Kinsey in *The Washington Post* indicated that the word "Buccaneers" should be eliminated as the name of the football team who just won the Super Bowl. In their opinion, this term represents violence. This article can be found in the outkick.com. This is just one of today's cancel culture indicators. Where does it stop?

From a sarcastic point of view, what if another media outlet wrote about their concern with the word "The"? That word is in the name of *The Washington Post*. Can any part of the media have and promote change of words for any reason? Should they be canceled or at least forced to change their name? Sorry for the sarcasm, but this has gone too far. Political correctness and cancel culture are way overused and could potentially cause more divisions in our country. The media often promotes cancel culture.

What if you are offended by the words "Washington" or "Post"—should you take a stand and talk about your opinion and demand to change those names for justice in the national arena? What are our media outlets doing to help unite us? If they cared about you, me, and America, that should be their focus.

Members of the media have grown to a point of believing they are superior to and more righteous than voters. Katie Couric on CBS stated that all people who voted for a different candidate for president than she and her TV station were advocating needed to be deprogramed. Katie Couric made the comment on the Bill Maher TV show in early January 2021. Do we the voters on all sides want to be told that we need mental help if we believe in a different way from others? China has reeducation camps to solve that issue. Is that where you want to go?

From a positive approach, we can stop listening to the false news. We will find fresh ideas to move our country forward, build a united culture, and give all Americans hope. All we get now is negative and partial truths that hinder positive attitudes.

They fill us with hate, sadness, and pain. We distrust our fellow Americans. The media, if left alone, will continue on a path to create many great divides in our society.

If you want a bright, successful future, please join this journey to get our representatives to hear us, answer us, inform us, respect us, and represent us. We need to open communication and stop the media and our government from separating and closing us off. We need to start to *Vote with Power*.

We deserve and must demand better and more accurate information. Our journey will provide the reason the media must change. If you want to help, go to www.votewithpower.com.

Chapter 5

Voters Have Privileges and Responsibilities

We have the country with the highest level of freedom, safety, mobility, and opportunities on earth. It is a privilege to live in and be part of America. For the most part we can live the lives we want. That is why millions of immigrants want to come to our country.

We live in a great nation that offers many types of freedom. One of the most important and critical freedoms is our right to vote. We need to be thankful and bless this privilege. We must keep our voting processes fair, accurate, and timely.

It is not just a right, but all Americans have a duty to vote and a duty to ensure their vote counts. Another duty we have, which we have been neglecting, is our voter duty to oversee our representatives. Once they are in office, our voter responsibility is not over. We must make sure they are doing the work for which they were elected/hired. Our responsibility is to hold them accountable for fulfilling their duties. We also have the privilege of setting up and using measuring tools to make sure they are staying active and promoting the best interests of all Americans. We currently lack the tools to track our representatives' activities and results. The journey you will read about in this book will supply those needed tools.

Would you hire a representative in Congress who does not spend their needed time on the job, those who would take your company in a different direction from the way you want them to proceed? Would you vote for candidates for the job in Congress who were going to create a culture of disrespect and delusions? Would you hire those who would not complete their tasks in a timely manner? Would you hire managers who would make radical, quick, and bad decisions? Would you hire them as employees, if you felt they would have major negative effects on our country? Your answer needs to be NO! In many cases, this is the way it is. We need to stop reelecting the wrong representatives. Often our voting decision is based on party not their voting record or what they have accomplished on our behalf.

This is what we are currently getting from many of the people we voted for and whose salaries we are paying.

We need to look at our representatives as employees. As their employers, we have the privilege of hiring, firing, and molding our representatives to represent us. Today we lack a means to do that. We have the responsibility to make sure they do what is in the best interests of our citizens and our wonderful country as we go into the future.

We must participate in our political process to promote and defend our democracy. If we fail to do so, we will lose our democracy. As a constitutional republic, our freedoms are provided by our democracy.

Our duty as voters is to make sure Congress stops totally voting along party lines. Our votes must count, or we are not being represented. We need to vote for those who will provide leadership and representation for all citizens of each state. Our representatives must pay attention to and promote our best interests. Vote for those representatives who have their constituents' interests in mind, not the candidates who say they will work with and for their constituents but fail to deliver. Those who act within their oath and work with and for us will be reelected. Our duty is to reelect those who represent us and remove those who do not.

Our responsibility as voters is to understand when our government is or is not working for us. We need to compare it to how our government should work for us. We need to analyze the current processes and decide whether they are functioning correctly on our behalf. We need to make changes in the current procedures. We need to be purposeful and create goals and plans to effectively get Congress to make the desired changes. This journey explains the way to make the needed process change. It is our privilege and duty.

We have another duty: to make sure our representatives are transparent and held accountable. If we are silenced, we will be under the direction of billionaires and super PACs, that is, those who are buying our elections. To fulfil this duty, we need to use an organized method of staying in touch with our representatives. The journey's prescribed two-way communication will help. This will keep the voters and representatives informed and involved. This should be a team effort. A new communication system ensures voters will have real power and have influence over our representatives. They will care more about how voters think and how they want to be represented. It is almost like the voters also need to take an oath to do their part, not just vote and leave. We need to vote and stay involved. Please vote and do your duty to help America.

This new voter engagement will work once enough voters get involved and work with Congress through this journey. This is a new way to perform the David and Goliath story. Instead of the voters (David) having to outsmart and use one weapon in a perfect way, we will retain our freedom by outgrowing the powerful Goliath. David won with one method; the voters will win using a different method. There are 535 members of congress and approximately 330 million Americans, who should have the power to direct our countries future?

If we fail to do more than merely vote, we will lose all the freedom and privileges we have. Our duty as Americans is to help guide our government, not just vote, and become silent. We need to stay involved in our government activities and decisions. We also should have more than 50 percent of Americans legally able to express their wishes by voting. If you do not vote, I say shame on you. You are missing one of life's biggest privileges.

I can never understand why 50 percent of potential voters in America fail to do so. Is it they do not care, they are too lazy, voting to them is inconvenient, or they do not think their vote will count? Those who do not vote need to understand that by not voting, they are voting against themselves. Their vote does count, and they need to use it if they care about their families and their future.

In America we are privileged to be on whatever career path we want, live wherever we want, own land and a home, own a business if we want, build the riches we want, get the education level we want, and have the freedom of expression and opinions we want. We also can travel where we want, have whatever hobbies we want, schedule our lives as we wish, have the good health care we want, and live in the safe neighborhood we want.

Besides protecting our freedoms, we need to protect and advance the above-mentioned freedoms for all Americans.

We must help our fellow citizens get what they want. Not by giving them money, but help. We have the responsibility to guide our representatives in protecting our freedoms. To see if we are being represented or not, we need transparency and accountability. Without using those tools, we will never be represented fairly.

We also have a duty to do our part by keeping our representatives informed on issues of interest and importance to us, in addition to how we see those issues. This new organization represented in this book will provide a means for our representatives to communicate with just a few voters and still get the opinions and thoughts of most of their constituents. The information shared with our representatives will not be judgmental, biased, or prejudiced. It will be the truth on how their constituents want them to proceed. Our voices will be heard through honest, open dialogue.

The information we communicate to our representatives will be consistent and timely. It will give voices to all their constituents who get involved. The purpose is to provide our representatives with all the information they need to do their job correctly. For those representatives who take part, there will be benefits. The voters will support our representatives who hear us, answer us, inform us, respect us, and represent us.

For those representatives who work within this new voter communication loop system, their job will become more comfortable. They will know what needs to be done and they will do it, and they will have the information from the voters and have job security. This change in representing the voters will alter the negative image our representatives have now. To stay in office, our representative will have to represent us, keep us informed, and tell us the truth.

This journey will help to improve their image. Members of Congress currently have a citizen approval rating of 15 percent, but they will be more respected and feel better as it grows higher. They will also be important to their voters as they will be placed on the right committees. Please commit to doing your part by voting and staying engaged in guiding your representatives. It is our civic duty. Your help will not take much time. It is critical to the future of all Americans. Let us *Vote with Power*.

For those who do not want to get involved, that is your privilege, but please stop complaining about our government if you are not willing to be part of the solution.

Chapter 6

Why We Need Leaders Who Will Run Our Country Differently

We need to vote for leaders who take their oath seriously and work within it to hear us, answer us, inform us, respect us, and represent us.

They need to tell us the whole truth and keep us informed. January 14, 2021, the president of our great nation was on national television telling us that his stimulus package was for the people. He was begging voters to contact their representatives in Congress, especially those from the opposite party, and try to convince them to vote for his stimulus package. He used an empathetic approach, telling the audience how important this bill was to them personally.

However, he neglected to tell us the whole story. He was hiding the truth about where most of the money was going. The bill represented a huge amount of money. He neglected to tell us where the money would come from. Go to *USAspending.gov* and you can be informed as to where our government is spending our tax dollars. *DAtalab.usaspendign.gov* shows the revenue and spending. According to that source, for the year 2020 the federal revenue was $3.42 trillion, and our federal spending was $6.55 trillion. Which means we spent $3.11 trillion more than we took in. According to the Congressional Budget Office the 2021 federal budget deficit will be $2.3 Trillion. (the source www.cbo,gov topics budget). That means any new spending legislation in front of Congress will have to be covered by borrowing or printing the money to fund this bill. Most of the funding will go to places of the president's party's interest. More of our children's financial future will go for political paybacks. Of the total budget ($1.9 trillion), in the stimulus package less than 9 percent was for Covid caused life destruction relief. This package was a typical party power bill. Instead of the small percent going to help individuals and businesses, most of the funds (91 percent) would flow to non-relief issues. $350 billion would go to municipalities that made bad budgeting decisions. Should we pay for their bailouts? In this bill was also a $15 an hour minimum wage. This, according to the neutral nonpolitical office of business and management, would cost millions of jobs. When high minimum wages are forced on businesses, they will raise their prices or cut their staff to remain profitable. The rest of the expenditure was hidden from us and going to the interests of the political party. This of course was without clarity and consideration of how we would pay for this huge expenditure. The president failed to address where the rest of the money was going. As if $1.35 trillion of our taxpayer money didn't matter to us.

The other side of the aisle attempted to fight this bill but had a difficult time due to the number of congressional seats held in both the House of Representatives and the Senate because their other party was outnumbered. This bill was full of pork spending. Only a small portion of the spending would go to help individuals and business. The other party was against the non-relief funding parts of this bill. This is an example of how politics works for the worse in our country. If you could tell your representatives how to vote on this package would you advise them to vote differently. They saw this money as funding that will have to be paid down the road by our children and grandchildren. Please, Mister President and members on both sides of Congress, tell us the entire truth. Where is your financial management responsibility? Where are your alliances and ethics?

If this were a business and not a government proposal, it would be viewed differently. It would fail to get approved. Is the $1.9 trillion spending or an investment? Some members of Congress claimed it will help the economy. It seems that this belief is a selling point to get the votes to pass the bill. Other experts claimed this will force inflation that will be disastrous for our economy.

Another salient issue from a business point of view is what other alternatives do we have to spending all that money on those personalized issues? How could the money be used in a better way?

Why don't we invest the $1.35 trillion not for Covid relief to get matching funds in communities that can set up funding for free college tuition? Check out what the past superintendent of the Kalamazoo, Michigan Public Schools set up with free college tuition for Kalamazoo Central graduates.

If this idea were considered and received matching funds, this would go a long way toward helping students who need financial support without having to go into heavy debt, and for those low-income students who are left out because they cannot even borrow money. Congress needs to focus on how else some of the spending could be used to have a positive effect for many years to come, not just a bailout for municipalities or be given to reward big money donors.

There are many other needs for those funds to help Americans that could have a lifelong impact.

We the voters need to help, oversee, and guide Congress so they stop wasting money on programs that are not working. Also, we need to stop those programs which only benefit a few people and yet cost millions of our tax dollars. Stop spending for paybacks and gifts. The Vote With Power communication loop system will have access to business-knowledgeable voters. They can assist in planning and developing implementation systems that help resolve the inequities. Our voice will help avoid more government-run, costly, unsuccessful programs.

In our new journey we will have input about where our government spends our taxpayer money and how much they spend. Their spending is obviously out of control. We need frugal representatives in Congress.

We need leaders who will stop crime and keep us safe. On February 7, 2021, the *Epoch Times* reported that there was a march in Washington, DC. It was mostly members of Black Lives Matter and Antifa. As they marched through the city, they were chanting, "Burn it Down." It was not stopped, silenced, or condemned by one party or most of the media. This type of behavior, if not stopped, will expand, and grow into more hate, more violence, and eventually take over our entire country. Our laws are there to protect us, but if these violent people are not held accountable, we will be heading back to the Wild West.

Does this behavior feel like freedom and safety for those who live in those neighborhoods? Answer that for yourself even if you do not live anywhere near Washington, DC. If left to grow, this behavior and trouble will be in your neighborhood soon.

We need to promote those who are skilled and interested in moving our country in the direction "we the voters" want.

Rational people operate from logic and define what they want to accomplish, why, and for whom. To keep a working relationship with spouses, children, coworkers, employers, and anyone in any organization, they find common ground. This helps with future decisions and progress for all. Through cooperation we can build a plan that will satisfy most voters.

We need leaders who will help build a relationship with their constituents that is in the best interests of the citizens who want to live in and promote democracy.

We need representatives who want to keep us and themselves informed. Obviously, our representatives cannot stay in communication with every voter. This book offers a plan for a way to not overburden them but share information they need from the voters.

We need leaders who want to get job satisfaction, build their self-worth, feel proud of their accomplishments, and get a feeling of confidence knowing they have helped unite us, those who will work with us and represent us. The only pride they currently feel, if they are honest, is from representing big money. Most leave office wealthy. How can you have career pride if you accomplished nothing, spent all your time promoting only the issues of your political party, failed to do your job, and have a low approval rating from those you are supposed to represent? Pride should not come from the trillions of dollars you gave as payback, especially since it was not your money. It was money you took from the citizens and will cause pain to our future generations.

We need leaders who will stop holding hearings with zero program changes. We need representatives who will do what they were elected to do, leaders who will work on bills that represent a high percent of American voters, not just their party. America needs to solve our problems and provide opportunities. America can be the land of the free, high income potential, good career opportunities, safety, educational opportunities, acceptance without racism or discrimination, fairness, and liberty for all.

These are examples of our dysfunctional government processes and actions that need changing.

1. Most legislation is voted on as a quick fix regulation for the sake of campaigning litany. The dysfunction here is too much emphasis is based on getting elected. We need Congress to start working on long-range goals to improve our nation and the lives of our citizens.

2. We need a federal government passing long-term legislation that will not need redoing within a few years. The dysfunction is that currently Congress does not operate based on future-oriented strategic plans.

3. Our federal government fails to spend enough time on paying off our national debt. Their focus is on politics. They are overspending and driving America into poverty. The dysfunction here is they do not know how to face or are not concerned about these major critical financial issues. They need our help in prioritizing their time and our money.

4. Congress avoids working on becoming more transparent and accountable. This dysfunction is the way to keep their power and avoid creating an operational system that will greatly enhance the lifestyles of all Americans.

5. Congress usually passes bills that are multi-issued, hundreds and even thousands of pages. These bills are often passed before they are fully read and understood. Do

they know what is in those bills? Or do they vote in the way their party wants them to? There is a famous statement that came out during the Affordable Care Act. The Speaker of the House of Representatives said, let us pass this bill and then find out what is in it. The dysfunction here is to pass the bill quickly before we find out what is in that bill. This is irresponsible and risky.

6. We need candidates who will stop telling us anything the polls indicate voters want to hear. That is currently how they get elected. The dysfunction here is that we do not hold them accountable for what they promise us to get votes. Candidates will say what they think they need to say to get elected. Once elected, they do what their party and lobbyists want them to do. Of course, they are constantly thinking about their reelection. When we get on this new journey, they will not have to spend most of their time positioning themselves to get reelected because the voters will have their voting records, activity, and performance reviews. Those who get high grades will almost automatically get reelected. Those who get low grades will be gone.

7. Congress needs to think about the consequences brought about by new legislation and regulations. The dysfunction here is that they do not see the big picture. They vote without taking responsibility for the future effects and results caused by the new legislation. Our representatives need to research and consider the long-term effects. They need to stop passing legislation just because it serves as a quick fix. An ongoing example is how Congress, every few months, votes to increase the cap on our huge national debt. They often pass a bill that keeps our government open. Where is this year's financial plan?

Where are the three- and five-year financial plans? They should address these issues with debt elimination in mind. Since they do not communicate with their voters, they fear cuts to spending and increasing taxes may cost them their jobs. We would help keep their jobs if they communicated with the voters and had good reasons for spending cuts and fair tax increases.

8. Congress often uses the technique of putting off issues by kicking the can down the road. Lack of working within a fiscally responsible budget is a good example of a critical area in which they are failing us.

Many of our representatives want us to sit down and be quiet. The representatives we elect in the future will want us to be involved to keep our independent thoughts and share valuable information back and forth with them. They are our employees, in a positive way, not a negative boss way. They will also have more independence as they communicate with voters and move away from the controls of their party and other influencers.

Many of the current representatives are arrogant and feel they are above us and that we need their decisions to protect us. They want to control the way we believe, think, and act in line with the freedoms they decide we are worthy of.

Congress currently, and for the past few years, has stopped listening to us, stopped answering our questions, and even worse, stopped representing us. This situation is getting worse.

Our representatives feel they know what we want and what we need. They make assumptions such as the high level of power they possess, or that it is their right to represent other entities over the interests of us the voters. Their assumptions are wrong.

From my college education in psychology, sociology, and a statistics course, I feel there is a truer picture of who they represent. I base my assumptions on thinking most voters fit into a bell-shaped curve, rather than a low-density high deviation plotting chart. Our representatives think we are so separated in values, beliefs, and thoughts that there will never be unity. This is what most politicians are counting on.

Do not take this bell-shaped curve assumption as fact. It is based only on my assumptions. It has not been proven or researched. This needs further research to see if it is true. But for the time being, it is practical, and I believe it will work for our journey.

From my perspective, the American voters' values and concerns fall on a bell-shaped curve. This means that 68.27 percent are close to the center of those who share core values. Those who want freedom, safety, representation, liberty, and the pursuit of happiness. This means that 68.27 percent of voters share those values, yet we are held hostage by the political atmosphere and the media, whose goal is to keep us divided. On a bell-shaped curve, most likely less than 3 percent of Americans are way radical on either the left or right ends of the continuum. This leaves 27.18 percent that move from the center out toward the extremists. Therefore, realistically if my assumptions are correct, there are roughly 81.66 percent of Americans who can unite and work together. They are more practical, honest, realistic, caring, law-abiding citizens. They just need a path and journey to bring them together. They will be flexible in giving and getting what is the best for all Americans.

In your business, would you pay your employees $174,000 a year if they failed to do the work they were hired for?

We currently elect persons we quickly find out we do not want. We fail to complete our due diligence through background checks. We do not vet them on having any leadership, management, business, or administrative skills. We do not even check their backgrounds for honesty unless we become aware that they have a federal offense on their record. We need to evaluate the candidates education, experience, experience, results, and cultural beliefs, and use other background screening processes before we vote for anyone.

The approval rating of Congress on a Gallup Poll at the time of this writing is 15 percent of approval, 83 percent of disapproval, and 3 percent with no opinion.

Would you retain employees in your business who only satisfied their performance standards 15 percent of the time?

Congress needs to understand and begin setting up processes and systems on some of the aspects of government that fit and will function like a successful business.

There are many important tasks and problems that our Congress spends little time on. They set their own priorities, often based on what rich doners want them to work on. They now vote on new laws and handle grievances. They also hold many hearings to fix problems. Many of the issues become power theatrics and nothing really gets done.

As a business coach, I am frequently reminded that 97 percent of small businesses in America never reach a high level of success. Around 80 percent fail within five years. These businesses fail due to spending all their time working *in* the business and not *on* it. Michael Gerber, years ago, wrote a fantastic book called *The E Myth*, which explained how to take a business into the future. In this case we need to have our leaders take our country and the good of the people into the future.

When do you see our government do future-focused strategic planning and build better communication systems to keep their employers (us) informed? They need to build a culture of unity, cooperation, and progress. What about creating across-the-aisle team-building processes? When do you hear of our government's year, three-year, and ten-year plans for our country? What is their mission and long-term vision for our country? Our Congress also lacks the discipline to set tracking and metrics to measure the progress and results from the changes they make though legislation. What have you read that indicates Congress is investigating new opportunities to make America better? What new ideas should Congress investigate?

When will our representatives complete a needed cash flow analysis and planning to prevent costly problems and stop wasting money? Where are our reserve funds for emergencies, repairs, and maintenance? They now wait until disaster hits and then allocate money we do not have to fix it. Take our infrastructure as one example. If we had the money available, we would make the repairs and replacements before they became expensive. Look at the condition of our roads, bridges, and other infrastructure. In your house, doesn't it make financial sense to replace the roof before the leaks ruin the boards and cost you more?

Is Congress investigating which of our systems, processes, laws, and bureaucratic rules are no longer needed or are harming businesses or citizens?

Life is more exciting, rewarding, and pleasing when you plan, work your plan, make positive change, and prevent problems before they exist. Motivation comes from finding new ways to improve your life every day. Now we are living in pain created by our dysfunctional government. We are living is a split culture society. How exciting and motivational is that? How do we help all Americans blend together and live peaceful lives?

The ideas in this book may seem radical to some people. Others will see these ideas as a way to greatly improve our lives. This process will take time and have many challenges along the way.

The dislike for our government is expanding each day. We need innovators who will work toward improving our government as we investigate the future. We can change attitudes if there is a reason to be motivated to do so. A negative response was there before the invention of the light bulb, the telephone, cell phones, and even computers. There are always naysayers who do not believe in any new programs. They can sit on the curb and watch the parade go past. That is fine with me, as I think most Americans want the changes expressed in this book.

In business every employee should have clarity of vision, passion, and understanding of how their efforts will help bring about the desired result. Congress does not have or use a bigger progressive vision. We need to help them with this problem. How do we look at our future and find new creative ideas, those that aren't even thought of today? Those that will improve our lives, liberty, freedom, and the pursuit of happiness?

We have the best country in the world, but where is the plan for fulfilling our dreams for the country we want in our future? In business, fresh, outside eyes are valuable to see a different big picture and the path that will move us forward. How many of our representatives are only living in the world they see? Especially when they are kept in congress for decades.

According to the preamble to our Constitution, the purpose of government is to establish justice, ensure domestic tranquility, provide for common defense, promote the general welfare, and work toward the advancement of liberty to each American.

Our current legislative branches are on different roads from each other and heading in different directions. They are trying to change the functions of our Constitution.

There is no cross-party cooperation. The media talks constantly about the aisle in Congress between the two parties. I do not see an aisle; I see white flags like an underground dog retention fence. If members of Congress get too close to the invisible fence, they will get zapped by their party.

We also need leaders who understand, respect, and want to help small businesses. Our representatives talk a good game of helping small businesses, but never walk the walk. Entrepreneurship is the stability, creativity, and growth of our economy through flexibility and ingenuity. Bureaucracy in this country kills off small business stability, growth, and business prosperity, along with the jobs it destroys. We need leaders who want to advance the growth of small businesses and will help promote business startups and prosperity.

On January 13, 2021, according to eguardian.com the senator Alexandria Ocasio-Cortez said on Instagram that she was close to death during the January 6, 2021, Capitol mob break-in. The problem for voters is that the dramatic way she expresses what she went through does not match the experience of the senator in the next office. It seems that the described event was not in the building or near the building of the break-in. We all agree the actual break-in was not acceptable and those invaders were criminals and need to pay for what they did. Is this leadership?

My concern is that we do not know the truth of the statements and theatrics of the senator who "feared for her life." The ongoing problem is that Congress has become so political and theatrical that they portray characteristics we do not want or can't afford in Congress.

The one situation I wrote about here is not the issue. But we see daily behavior from Congress on both sides of the aisle that is not acceptable and often close to illegal. Yet it goes on without retribution. Therefore, we the voters need a better system of truth, better screening of candidates, and stronger voices to eliminate the behaviors or representatives with those behaviors, whichever is needed.

Our new leaders will be driven by the serious and intense work they need to perform. No more acting to get attention. Do their job correctly and they will have our praise, gratitude, and attention, with new leadership styles that will improve our government and our lives. We must *Vote with Power*.

Chapter 7

Should Our Government Be Run as a Successful Business?

Most people do not look at our government functions as they would look at a business. Part of the functions of our government need to be looked in this light. In business, to be successful there needs to be people responsible for the results. To measure the results, there are several tracking systems in place.

I have been a business trainer and coach for many years. In this book I want to have you, the reader, get some ideas of how our government runs in comparison to how you should run a phenomenally successful business. You may already own a business or may someday own one. These comparisons and contrasts will give a different perspective of our government's weaknesses. They will point out the flaws and show how our government should function.

In addition to seeing the gaps in the way our representatives are approaching their tasks, I will make other contrasts and comparisons. We will also look at two different decision-making processes. Congress makes decisions in a way that is extremely different than how a successful business makes decisions. In most cases it should not be that way. Another area of concern is the difference in the approaches to handling challenges and making changes. It seems government approaches are not working, especially for the voters.

In business, every challenge must be met with the use of SMART goals, plans, leadership dialogue, processes, systems, and buy-in from all stakeholders. (SMART is an acronym meaning Specific, Measurable, Attainable, Relevant, Time-based.) Think about how Congress functions now. Do our representatives use commonly shared goals, strategic plans, defined purposes, or try to establish a consensus with the majority of their voters' views? The answer is no! This hinders our country's progress and works against building a better life for all Americans. Every day there are issues Congress should solve. With the intensity and thoughts of, "I am going to win at all costs, and you are going to lose," nothing gets accomplished. Plus, it makes for a future process lacking in communication and cooperation. It creates hate, mistrust, and deep desires to destroy their counterparts. Without voter intervention, nothing of good will come from this caustic atmosphere in Congress.

In our government there is no one responsible for tracking or measuring the results. Our representatives get away with the lack of planning or using a good decision-making model. This is due to us, the voters, failing to hold our representatives accountable or responsible. Our journey will rectify this.

All great businesses function within procedures, processes, and systems that they must follow to be efficient, productive, and get the results they want. They continue to use the systems that work well. Our government has rules (systems) that are often broken, and the processes change. Whichever political party is in office and has the political power they make changes to the systems and procedures of how they operate. Therefore, the business of government is inefficient and lacks consistency.

When Congress votes on bills, they do not use foresight or worry about ramifications. Their approach to get a bill passed is to talk with lobbyists and their party members to see how they should vote. They next plan what trades they must make to negotiate to get the other members of Congress to vote their way to get the bill passed. Their approach is not making plans to deal with issues but plans to get votes.

When business decisions are made correctly, they have a purpose and detailed plans. They will provide answers for the important questions: Who will be responsible for implementation and success? What processes and systems are needed to get the desired and expected results? What damages will be caused by or who will be hurt by this change? What will it cost and is it within budget? What are the short- and long-term desired results? Who should be included in the decision from a viewpoint of knowledge, skills, and experience? What information should be obtained before making any decision? Does everyone voting on this change have time to read and fully understand all components of this change?

Congress's approach is much more simplified. The problem is that it should not be that way. They work on passing a bill without taking the time and doing the research to answer the questions the way a successful business does. They do not consider the big picture, effects, or risks of what the citizens are getting or giving up. Once the bill is voted on and accepted, Congress considers its job done. You cannot consistently make good decisions if you are not responsible for the outcomes.

If you made a decision this way and did not look at all aspects, including the risks vs benefits, how long would you be in business?

Congress also works on urgent issues but tends to avoid the tough, important issues. If a business operated and focused only on the urgent issues most of the time, it would fail to progress and grow.

On January 28, 2021, Jen Psaki, the press secretary for President Biden was asked what the administration was doing about the Chinese Communist Party's aggressive military moves. She replied, we are in a mode of strategic patience. This article can be found in the Japantimes.co.jp. How can we sit back and watch China steal our technology, infiltrate our universities, build a stronger military than we have, and create relationships with members of our government? China's leaders have also made comments about taking over the world and destroying America. Is using strategic patience a comforting sound to us as Americans?

In business, if your competitors are coming after you with aggression, you would need to prepare to curtail their business-destroying activities.

To make more comparisons between businesses and our government, we need to look at the five critical footings to any successful business. (Sales/marketing, Finance, Human Resources, Leadership, and Operations. From the correct perspective, the same five should be addressed and followed to have a successful government.

The first foundational footing is sales/marketing. Congress needs to follow good business practices in these areas when they work on tariffs, trade agreements, and branding the right image of America. Our brand should be that of a friendly, caring, supportive country. We should not do our marketing and branding by framing us as a rich country that will provide other countries with all the money they need.

Another part of marketing/sales is to find ways to increase revenue, as a business must. This could be done through our government helping small businesses grow and prosper. As our businesses grow, there are many taxable events that produce tax dollars, which go to the government. Currently, our government is not using this strategy; instead, they are restricting and harming small businesses. Our government could become financial partners with small businesses, like venture capitalists or angel lenders. They would increase their revenue if they stayed out of the way. Let capitalism work naturally.

In the financial footing, as in business, Congress should work on balancing our assets with our liabilities. We need to get out of the debt quicksand we are in. Stop borrowing money we cannot pay back. We need to do what businesses have to do, such as projecting our cash flow needs and tracking and measuring our expenses. We need to find and plug holes through which money is being wasted. We need to get a fair return on investments made in groups.

We could increase government revenue by loaning our money instead of giving it away, but financial prudence does not allow us to print or borrow money to make loans. Even if we played the money spread game of borrowing the money at a low rate and loaning it out at a higher rate, this is dangerous. We are not in the banking business.

In the human resources footing, as I have written, we need to find, select, interview, and check the representatives we hire (vote for). Once we have the right representatives in place, we need to do performance reviews, keep them on track for meeting our needs, help them build a congenial culture, and build teams that work together.

In the leadership footing, Congress needs to develop strategic plans for handling conflicts and moving our country in the right direction. They need to develop processes that are in line with our mission. These should be based on our core values. True leaders get results, not just perform activities.

In the operations footing, processes are needed. Congress needs to set up communication systems that are based on gathering information from which to create agreement, cooperation, and flexibility, a process to work together. In a business, if all managers and leaders are heading in their own direction, the operation will be dysfunctional, and the business will fail. Our two-party system is not working because the two parties are not working together. We need them to work together.

How successful would your business be if your employees set their own schedules, set their own agendas, their own wages, their own vacations, and their own rules to live by? Would you allow them to spend all the money they want from your company? Use it for whatever they wanted and took your business in a direction you as the owner did not want? That is what we currently have in Congress.

In your business, what would you do with employees who presented the above behaviors? We need to get our representatives on our page. Their focus, interests, and activities need to be in line with ours.

We should never forget we elected (hired) our representatives. We cannot afford to just sit back and complain about what they are doing. We need to get involved and take action. In business, if you were the owner, you could promote yourself to the board of directors. That would be a shift in company responsibilities. You would let the new managing leaders (representatives) manage, administer, and operate the day-to-day business. You would make sure the managing leaders, COO, CFO, CEO, and president of your business, understand and work on fulfilling our mission. They would lead your company in the you have proposed. They should not have their jobs if they turn the company in a different direction. Our representatives need to stay on the path that delivers our mission, not theirs.

In business, the efficient way to operate is to only work on one critical issue at a time, while continuing to work on the day-to-day ongoing challenges and tasks. In our current government model, Congress is so fragmented they get nothing much accomplished. When they do solve a critical issue, it is after a fight over it and push it through at the last minute. In business, you cannot give up and finish a project just to get it done.

In business, every decision and change has consequences, good and bad. The way to prevent the negative effects or harm to the business is to solve the issues by use of plans before you make the changes.

In Congress, every decision and change has consequences, good and bad. The difference is that in business your consequences are on your shoulders. You are forced to live with what you decided and did. In Congress, they are not responsible for the consequences. They vote and they move on.

We the citizens of America pay the price. In the decisions of Congress, often some organizations get benefits while others are being hurt or treated unfairly. Businesses are very aware of the effects on all who might be affected by a given decision. In business, due to the critical outcomes, owners and executive teams need to do a lot more research, planning, anticipating results, and setting expectations whenever they make major decision or changes. In Congress, since the consequences do not come back to haunt them, they do not need to understand all the potential harm they are doing to the voters.

Our current operational system of government looks like this. There is lack of transparency and accountability. This rewards representatives who are working for big money. They get rewarded by donations for their reelection.

Members of Congress have few consequences for not representing the voters because they get their reward from big money, in the form of more money and benefits.

We need leaders who are watchdogs over the advancement of huge money and power growth. The recent growth of the Big Tech monopolies is having a bad effect on America. Congress's cooperation gives Big Tech the ability to crush our freedom of speech and protects them from competition. This needs to be controlled and dealt with.

We need to reconstruct the way Congress operates. Congress has gotten so politically driven it is really upsetting to most Americans. That is why we need to *Vote with Power*.

Members of Congress make decisions based on rewarding three different thought patterns. They vote the way of the voters, vote from their own judgments, or they vote from the desires and influence of entities outside our government.

We need to make sure they stay on track with our beliefs and desires and that they act in our best interests. If they make decisions from their own judgment, they need to inform us and justify their behavior.

The current legislative process fails to stay focused on protecting our freedom and our democratic system. Congress often provides what they think are good solutions to problems in America. Their approach is not working. Most of the time, they make changes to solve problems that end up making worse situations for many people. Congress needs a business model for handling conflicts and advancing our rights, the rights of all Americans.

A bill can originate in either chamber of Congress, except for a revenue or appropriations bill. Those must start in the House of Representatives. Any member or group of members of Congress can bring a bill to the chamber. Congressmen and -women can initiate a bill based on their own initiative or from the influence of any group or person.

Once introduced, the bill is sent to the appropriate committee where members will debate and often redraft it. During this process, many congressional staff members play a critical role.

The process should be changed to allow either a single issue or similar issue legislation only. No more complex legislation, full of unrelated topics. An example is found in the Affordable Care Act, which is full of a multitude of new rules, regulations, and laws, many of which have nothing to do with health care. This bill contained thousands of pages and was passed in a few days.

During this stage, we need a new communication loop to take place, so Congress does not get only the opinions and influence from big business, political parties, and strong special money interests. This is where the public communicates and has equal representation along with all other factors.

Bills, after clearing the committee, get put on the docket in the house where the bill originated. There, all members of that house will debate it. More amendments and changes are made until eventually it comes to a vote.

At this stage, a neutral agency representing the voters should check to ensure the legislation falls within the budget and is constitutional. It is also important that spending projection totals are agreed upon by both parties and there is no more "fuzzy math" increasing the lack of transparency. The predictions and forecasts of spending need to be based on both parties agreement on using the assumptions and dollar totals. The research assessment from the CBO (Congressional Budget Office) should come into play at this time.

Before voting on a bill, we need to have all members of Congress pledge they have read the bill and fully understand the impact it will have on the people.

Bills, when passed, go to the other chamber, and go through changes and amendments again. The bill will go back and forth with ongoing amendments and changes until both houses pass identical versions of the bill. Once passed by both houses, it goes to the President for his approval or veto.

During this stage of the process, as the bill goes to the President, every bill needs to be researched to make sure it defines who will be responsible. That is in addition to making sure the laws can realistically be implemented and include a system providing for a follow-up approach to ensure someone is responsible and accountable For implementation, watchdog on the funds and success.

We need to require that all legislation provides a synopsis filled out on a transparency form, so we the people can easily understand the source, magnitude, purpose, and the short- and long-term costs, as well as who benefits, who—if anyone—might be harmed, and whether there is a better alternative. Another check is to see whether this legislation falls within the guidelines of the budget and the Constitution of the United States.

Legal bribery through unlimited campaign PACs and gerrymandering to stack the political deck gives unfair party benefits in either passing or thwarting legislation. New regulations and transparency, along with an oversight system, need to correct this situation.

The book written by Peter Schweizer titled, *Extortion, How Politicians Extract Your Money, Buy Votes, and Line Their Own Pockets,* is a good read and will shock you with what is happening in our legislation process. One of the points of *Extortion* is how bills get bought out of committee. They can stay in committee for ever. The Speaker of the House has the power to decide which bills and when, they will come out of committee. This is a use of power to influence legislation. Mr. Schweizer, who has experience in Congress, has written about this. Big business or banks who have an interest in getting a bill out of committee and voted on for their benefit have a way to donate money to the party that has the power to get their legislation of interest moving forward. Bills that represent small organizations or the public will be kept low on the priority list. The book points out that both parties in the House of Representatives are guilty of demanding party dues beyond those they raised for the individual politician. The hidden agenda is that representatives selected for committees and subcommittees are often not the ones with the highest qualifications. Their selection is based on how much money that representative can bring into the party. To read more go to pages 62 – 66 in Peter Schweizer's book, Extortion.

We must change this approach of selecting congressional committee members by who raises the most funds. New voter input and oversight are needed to develop a new process for selecting committee members and committee heads by qualifications. These changes would give the power back to the people to have a government of the people, for the people, and by the people.

We also need to make sure those representatives who are committee heads and run subcommittees have leadership skills. A few years back, Congress was getting concerned about the declining middle class in America. A committee was put together to research how to advance the growth of our middle class. The selection process was interesting because all members of that committee where in income levels above middle class.

Doesn't it make sense to lead by using citizens from the middle class to at least provide input? Better yet, to be on that committee or, best of all, lead that committee?

Our committee operational systems should be changed. If a bill has merit, why do we always have arguing, name-calling, grandstanding, and outright obnoxious behavior? Where is the professionalism, listening, idea sharing, and voting for the rights of the people? There will always be disagreements, and that is healthy. But already deciding on how to vote before reading or understanding the thousand-page bills is ridiculous.

Are the representatives thinking of their constituents first? The answer is no! I have a question for the voters. For those in Congress who vote 95 percent or more along party lines, why do we pay them?

It would be much cheaper to put a note on their desk that says, "I vote for whatever my party wants me to vote for. I vote no on any issue the opposite party wants." This would save us $174,000 a year, times the number of representatives who vote strictly along party lines.

When it comes to trade agreements, the negotiation process should always be fair to all countries, including the United States of America. Our leaders for years have given American benefits away so the weak negotiators can be seen as nice people. In successful negotiation the atmosphere must be set for the desired results. This is true in many areas of our lives. During my first year of teaching, I was more interested in being liked than respected. The price I paid was the loss of control of the classes. I learned quickly and changed my priorities. I found that if I gained respect, I was happier. The class wasted little time on discipline. The students were learning more. The side benefit was that I was highly liked. Our negotiators need to be respected. These critical business transactions make American businesses billions or lose American business billions of dollars. We must keep the interests of the American economy, our businesses, and farmers paramount, without bullying or cheating other countries.

In the past, Congress rarely considered building cooperation between our government, American privately held businesses, and the military. In essence, this means to build a team with members from both the public and private sectors to promote the productivity and efficiency or the issues we need to solve.

One of the few examples of cooperation is Operation Warp Speed program, which greatly improved the development and distribution of the COVID-19 vaccine. Most Americans cannot come up with another good example of a cooperative venture between our military, private industry, public funds, and government agencies. This joint venture idea could take advantage of private funding, volunteers, and corporate logistics knowledge to create fast and high-quality successful programs. This could have great advantages and new opportunities, however guarded against government favors.

We need this success to use as an example to emulate and frequently use cooperation from all resources in the future to handle problems and provide opportunities.

There are eleven major changes we need to make to fix our government:

1. Implement the voters' journey and organization advocated in this book.
2. Have candidates, whether incumbents or newly elected legislators, sign a commitment letter. This letter would include pledging the following:
   A. I will keep active communications with the Vote With Power new state centers and share information by

being in the loop. The centers referred to here, are explained in this book. They will create a communication loop between the voters and the representatives they elect.

B. I will approach legislation with common sense, with a cooperative and compromising attitude.

C. I will only vote for bills that contain single and related issues.

D. I will not vote for bills containing legal bribery such as pork to get them passed.

E. I will not vote for any bill that I have not read or that I don't understand.

F. I will keep the best interests of my constituents higher than my political party's interests, or the attempted influence of lobbyists.

G. I will fight to stop using gerrymandering as a tool to get political gain.

H. I will not vote for any legislation that is not within my power as given through the Constitution of the United States of America.

3. We must only fill positions of department heads, agency leaders, and cabinet members with people who have the experiences and qualifications for that position. We need to stop the payback system for paying back campaign money and favors.

4. We must force Congress to use accurate financial forecasts obtained from nonpartisan research such as the Congressional Office of Management and Budget and agree on the forecast figures to stop all fuzzy math. This would give the voters true numbers, not political party projections that are millions of dollars apart.

5. We must get congressional candidates to agree to avoid the use of unproven or out-of-context information. Stop presenting the other candidate or party in an untruthful light. We need to start only voting for candidates when we know what they stand for. What accomplishment have they attained? No more stone throwing so we vote against a candidate, rather than for who will represent our best interests.

6. We must get Congress to focus on important issues and take the time to research and establish solutions on a long-term basis. Thus, stop kicking the can down the street and wasting our money and time.

7. We must get congressional leaders to vote only for legislation that comes with plans for implementation, and provides responsibility for implementing that plan, including being accountable for the frugal use of appropriated money.

8. We need to get Congress to approve only legislation that is within the budget.

9. We must hold Congress accountable for **auditing** the bureaucratic agencies to make sure each agency is cost-effective, efficient, necessary, and to ensure there are no agencies with overlaps and gaps in their responsibilities. We must ensure that no bureaucratic entity has too much power.

10. We must set up systems whereby the public is informed of campaign promises made and the actual results obtained by the candidate after they were elected. No longer will candidates tell us what they will do and then not do it. The journey's performance review process will guard against faking results.

11. We must dilute the power and influence of special interest groups, big tech, and big business money.

We need to get candidates and elected representatives to commit to telling us the whole truth. At the time of this writing, As previously mentioned, Congress is in the middle of a COVID-19 relief bill. The majority of the $1.9 trillion does not go for any COVID-19 relief. Most of the money is political paybacks and gifts to friends. We the people have been asked to support this bill. Most voters will be getting a $1,400 one-time relief payment. Congress forgot to tell us that if you live in Washington, DC, you will get $400 weekly. How is that fair and good use of our hard-earned tax dollars? One proponent of this bill stated that 70 percent of Americans approve of passing this bill. That comment came from a member of Congress. Those Americans either do not understand the full spending in this bill or they only want to pass this bill to get their $1,400. Do we Americans really want government handouts? I say yes to hand-outs for those who were negatively affected by the pandemic, but not to the general public. The $1,400 will cost all of us more than that in interest and/or raised taxes and increased debt for our future generations, who will have the burden of paying off trillions of dollars in debt balance and interest. Any American who cares about our country cannot see how spending $1.9 trillion without regard to the effects on our future generations is acceptable. That representative who said Americans approve of the bill knows the voters would not want to get this bill passed if they had the whole truth. The voters need to help Congress prioritize the money-spending plans. We have a better reason for using our money properly to help all Americans.

Congress, to be successful and represent us, must start to make decisions and vote on legislation by using defined purposes, goals, planning, tracking, and being responsible and transparent.

It does not matter if you are a liberal, conservative, democratic socialist, Democrat or Republican. We need to stop the way Congress is operating. We need to share ideas and come to agreement on the issues and the direction our country is heading. This can only be accomplished when we begin sharing truthful, honest information. Our opinions and ideas approach, which is explained in this book, will help close the divide through an inquiring and cooperative spirit and a paradigm shift for all to win together.

Let us look further into the way a successful business would approach handling the border immigration problems.

We cannot just open the borders to everyone and anyone who wants to live in our country. Just from housing, job, and cost needs, it is easy to see we do not have the resources to let in all who want to enter our country.

If you get pressured to believe in totally opening our borders, ask the person challenging you if they still want open borders if they had to take twenty immigrants to live in their home, pay for their health care, get them jobs, feed them, and pay for their education. Most voters do not have the resources to provide those services.

Since we have stopped vetting people coming into our country, we don't have any control over the quality, health, criminal backgrounds, or culture of the people becoming our neighbors. A vetting process is needed to set up and provide decisions for qualifications and disqualifications for entry into America. We want people to come to America but not everyone!

This causes other problems, such as migrants with contagious diseases, or criminals, sellers of drugs, gang members, or human traffickers. Others without those problems may cause other negative situations due to lacking the skills, education, language, or ability to ever assimilate into America. Some could never be productive or contribute to our society. We cannot afford that burden. We must vet and only let in those who only need short-term minimal help. We want to welcome and help people come into our country and become American citizens. We must be mindful of preventing danger to our citizens and avoid taking risks.

On the other side, we do not want to exclude those we approve of from getting into our country. There must be a reasonable number of people per year. We must close the border temporarily. Decide who, how many, what qualifications are needed, and from where we let in. Next set up an efficient vetting system. This puts us back in control and yet should meet our countries goals.

To solve the immigration dilemma, we need to set goals and establish guidelines. Just as an example, how many people from Mexico can we agree on letting in during the next twelve months? Can we set a goal, maybe 200,000 per year for the next five years, and watch the progress? We could let in hundreds of thousands of immigrants we are not prepared to handle or help. That would be bad for our country and equally bad for those coming into our country.

We cannot appease the few people who think we should freely let all immigrants, as many as want to, come to America. If we are overwhelmed, it will lower the standard of living for Americans who are already here. We should not give up our quality lifestyles or future opportunities as a gift to anyone who wants what we have.

Other standards could include requiring them to answer questions before they come into our country. Research will determine if they will be an upstanding person of value to their community and identify those who seriously want to become American citizens.

We need to set standards for vetting. Examples could be education, job skills, their potential to be model citizens, and the ability to be self-sufficient and to contribute to our society. An application process should be utilized and received before people start their journey to our country. This process would save lives, be fair, and avoid the burden of thousands of immigrants coming to America, especially those who are not qualified.

We would then draw up a plan for when they enter our country. How will we support and track them and help them get jobs, work toward their citizenship, find housing, fund them, and pay their health care and education until they get a quality job and are self-sufficient?

We would not be policing the immigrants but helping them and making sure they do not follow a path to crime or a gang lifestyle. Currently we pretty much let them in and turn them loose to be responsible for their own survival unless they have sponsors.

We are not all going to agree on the level of restrictions and qualifications for entry, but it would start a dialogue and we would reach some agreement on common ground through common sense. It would start to work, which is better than not agreeing. Our current blame and bickering system will continue to hinder our ability to put together a working, balanced immigration system. This is another example of kicking the can down the street. Congress has said for years we need immigration reform, but what has been accomplished? The way we are letting immigrants in now, we are taking high risks, hurting the immigrants', and potentially lowering the quality of life and raising the safety risk of American citizens.

Put this in perspective within your life. If you wanted a driver's license, you would have to qualify; if you wanted to get into a college, you would have to qualify; if you wanted a certain job, you would have to qualify; if you want freedom, you must behave in a certain way. Likewise, if you want to live in America, you have to qualify.

When you want to buy life insurance, you have to qualify. Why is it so horrendously demeaning to have immigrants qualify to get into our country? To become a citizen, they will have to qualify. That is the way of life in America, which we all need to appreciate and respect. I for one am glad we have hoops to jump through. If we did not make decisions on who comes to America, we would be operating without a well-designed and functioning system. We would have no rules. This is not fair to immigrants and—even worse—not fair to the American citizens.

To improve the current system, we need to remain calm and rational. Find common ground with goals, purpose, and plans. We can dialogue to learn everyone's thoughts, ideas, and why they think the way they do. This changes the atmosphere and moves us away from dogmatic beliefs and closing discussions. Understanding other positions is the only way to cooperate and move forward. No one will get their way all the time. Working while learning from each other will bring about congeniality, unity, and results.

If vetting is not done correctly, by plan and with purpose, we will begin to have health, economic, safety, language, and cultural problems.

Can we agree that we need goals, plans, and a vetting system to secure our safety?

With this new journey we will be sharing truthful and honest information. Our opinions, and ideas will have value. This book will explain this new approach to regaining voter influence. We need to work together. We share more lifestyle wishes than we can afford politics to divide us. We need to stop the way Congress is functioning now. We are allowing those far right and far left factions, plus big money, big tech, and the media, to destroy our country and our freedom.

Why don't we work to help others get the same American benefits we want? Why is Congress not concerned about voters' welfare as much as the interests of others? They are playing the "divide and conquer" game.

The mission of our government is to serve the American public, keep us safe, give us liberty and opportunities, and a good life. The best way to do their duty is to start using business models and processes.

Our representatives will need us to *Vote with Power*. Then we need to support them through training in thinking and functioning differently. Once we add our communication loop centers which have the purpose for gaining transparency and accountability to guide the voter focus from our representatives, America will progress in the right direction for all. We will all be safer and happier and have the opportunity to live with peace of mind.

Chapter 8

The Test!

The voters must answer the following question: **What do we need from our representatives before we elect them?** Every business uses resumes and research to have enough information to decide who to hire. Have you ever seen a resume from any candidate running for office?

There is one question all human resources directors ask candidates, especially in the upper income level jobs: **What can you bring to the table to help our company?** Do we as voters ever ask that question?

When considering passing bills, we need answers to accept moving forward with legislation. The questions listed below need to have answers.

Is this a one-issue bill with maybe only a few related issues? Or are there many bills bundled together?

Is this bill in the best interests of the American people first?

Does this bill relate to our purpose of government in helping Americans be better off in the areas of life, liberty, and the pursuit of happiness?

Is the money we are about to use an expense or an investment? If investment, what return can we expect?

Can we afford this bill under our current budget? Where will the money come from?

Can you justify the reason for spending the money, and how will we pay for it? Do we need to print it or borrow it?

How will our representative's vote be in line with their responsibility and authority, given to them by their oath of office?

Will this bill help the needs of hardworking citizens and assist them in building character and a life of opportunity and happiness, or is it just a gift to someone else in America?

Should this money be invested and used for American prosperity or is it a gift to foreign entities?

Do the representatives know what their constituents want for a particular bill?

Do our representatives know what parts of the bill or total bill their constituents do not want passed?

Is it in the best interests of most of their constituents?

Is their vote based on truth, knowledge, and fact or "vote and find out what is in it later"?

Where is the pressure coming from to get this bill passed?

Do both parties respect each other's opinion on this bill, and will they communicate in a positive, caring, helping manner?

On this legislation, are our elected officials trying to pass it without voters' input? If so, why?

What have you as my representative done in the last six months to advance our economy, small businesses, our safety, our freedom, our culture, our income, our opportunities, our health, and our overall freedom?

Will the representatives reach out to their voters for input or not?

Will Congress answer our questions honestly or not?

Are our representatives accomplishing the issues we sent them to Washington to resolve? Are they making our lives better?

Do our members of Congress really want to be held responsible or not?

What is the motive, purpose, and expected good to come from our representative's vote on this issue?

Do our representatives operate from our point of view? Do they approach their job from their parties' point of view?

Here are some additional questions we need answered before our representatives vote on legislation.

1. What is the legislation's purpose?
2. What are the goals and expected results?
3. What is your plan for implementation?
4. Who will be responsible?
5. How will the results be tracked?
6. Are there better uses for the money or better alternatives for this bill?
7. Were the above answers from our representatives shared with their constituents before they voted on the bill?
8. Would they vote the same on these issues if they weren't influenced by their party?
9. Who will benefit from this bill and who will it potentially hurt?

This business decision model is needed to change the landscape of how legislation is passed currently. This format would bring logic, common sense, and voter representation to the forefront.

Here is a sample of a performance review questionnaire. After being improved, it could be used to assess the voting and performance track record of our representatives.

1. What have you done within the past six months to improve America?

2. What have you initiated in the past six months to improve the lives of American families?

3. What have you accomplished in the past six months to provide more and better job opportunities?

4. What have you accomplished in the past six months to advance our economy?

5. What have you done in the past six months to ensure Americans' safety?

6. What have you accomplished in the past six months to help the low-income and poverty-stricken individuals to help them gain self-confidence, hope, education, and move away from relying on government assistance? What have you done to promote a healthy family structure in the underserved areas?

7. What have you accomplished in the past six months to ensure we are functioning within the national budget?

8. What have you accomplished in the past six months to implement plans and take action to lower the debt?

9. What have you accomplished in the past six months to ensure American freedom?

10. In the last six months, how much time have you spent name-calling, bashing, or belittling members of the opposite party?

11. How many times in the past six months have you voted to go along with your party instead of using your best judgment and input from your constituents?

12. What in the past six months have you initiated to help build unity in America?

13. What have you done in the past six months to improve your behavior to be more transparent, accountable,

and cooperative with the other party? How have you looked at the centrist point of view during your decision-making efforts?

I belonged to the Rotary Club years ago. I wish everyone would live according to and promote the Rotary Club pledge. The Rotary chapters have been using it since 1943. It states, "Of the things we think, say, or do: is it the truth? Is it fair to all concerned? Will it build goodwill and better friendships?"

If Congress would adapt this philosophy to focus and act on, it would help unite Americans. To help our representatives become aware of their behaviors and how they relate to voters' needs, we need a system. Our journey and organization will help track the voting records and performance guidelines. The representatives will have the tools to easily keep in touch with voters' opinions and expectations. Without this, the trend of dysfunction will continue, and in that case, we are not getting our $174,000 a year value.

Chapter 9

Short- and Long-Term Needed Governmental Changes

We need to remove the power of big banks, big corporations, big lobbyist groups, big tech companies, big individual money, political party affiliation, and even foreign influence. This will be a hard road to accept for all those entities and our representatives who enjoy the current situation.

Our long-term goal is to get rid of the influence and power of money and change it to the wishes of the American people.

Congress holds the cards for all the above influencers. The problem is that members of Congress are the ones with the power to change the existing model. Since this model fits their comfort zone, they have no reason to change.

Since members of Congress are in charge of making the changes on this issue, changes are a long way off!

There are some short-term activities to start to correct this situation. These will help to return the power, attention, and results to the people (voters). The short-term plans will accomplish this by setting up transparency and accountability centers, one in each state. These will be the communication loop centers. We must build the strength of influence over the representatives back to their constituents. The level of influence must be strong enough to offset the representatives' interests and willingness to act on behalf of other entities, such as those who gave huge donations to help win campaigns.

Another long-term goal is to have laws that protect our country and every individual's financial well-being. We need to make it unlawful to add pork and billions of dollars to bills that are not initiated for that purpose. The current trade of huge amounts of overbudgeted monies is destructive to our financial health. These monies are going all over to reward heavyweight influences. That donated money is used to buy votes to get representatives elected. The large amounts of donated money could be used for philanthropic good. It could be used to provide benefits for needed projects and citizens who need help. Does $140 million to build an underground transit system in Silicon Valley bring this to light? Big tech is getting a gift.

A short-term solution to this financial corruption is to get the voters involved and for them to understand what is happening. Voters then can provide their opinion and influence their representatives to stop passing bills or parts of bills that add to our huge growing national debt. Voters must demand single-issue bills only. Future bills must be funded within the budget.

Another short-term objective is to weaken the influence of donations in exchanged for payback. This could be accomplished by placing legal low level capped limits on donations from any and all individuals and organizations.

A long-term goal may be to develop and implement a system of election funding from our budgeted federal money. This would take some intense work to be representative and fair. It would be fiscally responsible, limited, and provide for a level playing field for all candidates.

Another long-term goal is to have Congress understand what activities and tasks in their job description they need to focus on. They need to manage those duties that align with best business practices. Our representatives need to become financially responsible and good money managers.

These best business practices include budgeting, safety protection, reduction of debt, supporting law and order, spending controls, representation of their constituents, customer (constituent) satisfaction, and cooperation with other members of Congress. Representatives need to stop listening only to their own party members. These can all be set as goals, and we need metrics to measure efforts and results. Members of Congress will get their voting records and the voters performance reviews. They will be graded. They will know where they stand with their constituents.

The short-term activities here are to set up the journey's polls, surveys, and questionnaire to gather voter information.

Another long-term goal is to get those running for office to be honest, open, and state their platform and expected results they want to accomplish. They will do their best to get those results if elected by our votes. Then for those who get elected, we need to track their activities, voting record, and results record. We can then match it to what promises they ran on. Did they run on the truth, the whole truth of their plans? We need to know which ones we voted for who fed us false hope, bashed their competitors, and delivered nothing of value to their constituents.

As a short-term activity, we must start voting only after we have gathered more information on the candidates. Without honest, detailed information on candidates, we often vote for someone who will not represent our interest and who doesn't have any plans to make our lives better. Without more information, we do not know what candidates really stand for and what and who they will represent once elected. We vote against someone because of what we heard about the candidate from bad sources, such as the media and the other political challenger. We get a slanted view from the negative comments and adverse advertising, which condemns the candidate without true facts or representation. Our candidates will have a different view of their job as they will know their voting records and performance will be tracked and shared.

In the long term, we need to cull the herd of those in Congress who do not represent us and those who accomplish nothing.

A short-term activity is to set up the transparency, accountability, and communication loop centers. The information gathered and shared from the centers will give voters a complete picture of what and who their representative is working for. The representative who came into office and stayed within their oath will be rewarded. Unwanted legislators who did not perform as expected can be voted out at their next election. For a few bad members there are ways to pursue getting them out of office before their next election, but this will be a challenging, slow process. Especially as parties protect their own even when they committed bad behavior.

Another long-term goal is to elect those who are passionate and committed to hear us, answer us, inform us, respect us, and represent us.

We need to start voting for candidates who have good ideas, plans, strategies, and solutions instead of personalities, parties, or huge advertising budgets.

Another short-term goal is to gather more information and demand candidates tell us what they want and think they can accomplish. They need to know their campaign promises will be tracked with the transparency and accountability centers. This should persuade anyone who has a hidden agenda or no plans for accomplishing anything for their constituents to think twice about running.

A crucial long-term goal is to move all Americans out of poverty, off the streets, and away from drugs. This can be accomplished through the right programs, with some investment. This can be accomplished by creating the right culture, building families, providing educational opportunities, and making mindset changes. With the use of good mentors for career and life coaches, individuals will gain hope, self-awareness, and the dream to become whatever they want and build the lifestyle they deserve.

It will not happen overnight.

The short-term approach is to get the do-gooders to understand that providing unconditional welfare to the people does not work. It keeps people in poverty and lowers their motivation and hope for a better life. We need to create plans to help struggling people who have potential to get what they need as long as they are showing personal growth. What we have been doing is throwing money at low-income people without expectations. This has not and never will work. Without offering low-income people the right tools and inspiring them to take on responsibility for their own growth, we are wasting money. We are actually pushing them into a deeper hole. To help people change and improve their lives, we need to give them hope, guidance, trust, and a plan, along with mentors to keep them focused and on track. We need to address their self-confidence, attitude about their children's education, hope, personal confidence, their family structure, and their attitudes, and promote positive attitudes and solid families, as well as helping them have a passion to take the help and build on it.

We need to stop feeling sorry for and guilty about those in need. Welfare in most cases harms those who get it, except for those who have disabilities and lack the emotional, mental, or physical attributes to become productive. There are some who need financial support only because of disabilities, and that's fine. We should provide them with financial assistance. However, we do not need to give only financial support to those who have potential. We need to educate and offer programs that build a path to self-worth, prosperity, self-esteem, career opportunities, and personal growth.

The do-gooders will not understand their concept of welfare is a waste, until they have to personally write the checks while people with potential sit on their couches. Note, I am not referring to the unfortunate Americans who for many reasons lack the capacity or potential for growth.

The main long-term goals are to get both houses of Congress to work through new legislative processes with a single purpose, separate from multiple issues that do not go together. This will advance transparency, give the American people a way to understand what is being done, and keep the pork trading and waste out of the process. Congress needs to learn to negotiate from a new vantage point. They need to improve their sales skills to help the people they represent, explain why a particular bill is valuable to them, and then answer what merits the bill and the associated expenditure have for America. Not the current system of, "I will give you a pork sandwich if you give me an even bigger pork sandwich." It won't stop until voters take a position. It is the system.

If we the American people want a pork sandwich, we must earn it. If those in Congress want a pork sandwich, they just take money we do not have or print some.

The short-term activities we need to perform are: We will communicate frequently with Congress and show our disappointment for any overbudget or wasteful spending.

In business, we do not like most salespersons approach, but we do like to buy. The difference is a top salesperson listens and fits the value to the wants and needs of the prospect—not shove items down our throats, as Congress often does. Would you accept giving up your grandchildren's hope of a happy, safe, free, wonderful economic life, or would you rather have the discipline and ability to determination what research programs receive your taxpayer funding? Many projects or programs receiving taxpayer funding would not be accepted by most Americans if they knew about those programs. To many people, these expenditures are a waste of money. Taxpayer dollars should not be funding programs or research that only reward a few people and don't improve the majority of American lives. It is taxpayer money, and the voters should have the right to help set spending priorities. A recent example was our government gave a grant of thousands of dollars to research how long it takes a panda to poop. Did that result help America and your life? In an article written by Paul Tracy updated on January 16, 2020, listed 6 Projects you won't believe the government is funding. Check it out at investinganswers.com.

1. A snow making facility in Minnesota – cost $6 million.
2. Rearranging desks at the SEC Offices – cost $3.9 million.
3. The renovation of 37 rural bridges in Wisconsin – cost $15.8 million
4. Improving Energy Efficiency in a Tennessee mall – cost $5 million.
5. A pizza machine in San Jose – cost $720,000.
6. A turtle tunnel in Florida – cost $3.4 million.

There are hundreds of more examples every year. Did any of those projects help solve America's critical problems?

A long-term goal is to unify our nation, to reduce and eliminate the hate, misunderstanding, prejudices, unbalanced law enforcement, blaming, name-calling, and power grabs that have divided our country to a point of total dysfunction. The long-term goal is to rebuild our nation, our government, our core values, and our cooperation, even in the face of disagreement.

The main short-term activity we need to carry out to start increasing our unity is to begin hearing each other, answering each other without judgment, and understanding the desires of the majority of American people. And we need to stop being pushed in all directions based on politics. Let us Americans start the dialogue through the transparency and accountability centers. This will help us understand and share our individual wants and needs. This communication loop system will promote unity and concern for others' wants and needs. It will gain in understanding and civility toward the priorities of all Americans. From there we will have a shared philosophy. This will stop the media, big tech, and our politicians telling us what they want us to know and not know.

A fundamental long-term goal is to solve all our current major problems and the political divisions hindering the approach we need to have and the decisions that need to be made.

There is a big political divide that needs to be corrected soon.

These are the issues both party leaders tell us we need to stand for. Do they really know?

1. Big government vs small government.
2. Medicare/Medicaid for all.
3. Open borders.
4. College tuition free for all.

5. Legalized sanctuary cites.
6. Paid health care and unemployment for illegal aliens.
7. Socialism vs. Capitalism.
8. Defund the police.
9. More consistent and fair enforcement of our laws.
10. No bail and immediate free release policies of caught suspects, even those considered high crimes. The Attorney Generals in California and New York have taken this position to let suspected criminals go free without paying bond. The news continues to give examples when these low- level offenses and even some felony cases. criminals are released to commit crimes soon after their release. According to a fox news published article written by Lois Casino on February 22, 2021 states have recently enacted bail-reform laws. Criminal courts are prohibited from taking cash bail. States such as New York, California, and New Jersey have taken steps to ban the practice of using cash bail.
11. Free enterprise so Americans can build wealth vs. high taxes to redistribute wealth.
12. Higher taxes vs. keeping taxes at a reasonable level compared to personal needs and fairness.
13. Increasing vs. decreasing the bureaucracy.
14. Spend time and money on climate control vs spend nothing, as we have little effect on climate change until China and India do their part. We have been lowering our admissions.

The short-term activities we need to carry out are to get our *Vote with Power,* open the accountability and transparency communication loop offices prescribed in this book. These offices will be a source for discussions among the voters about which of the above listed problems they need to prioritize. The information gleaned from the discussions will then be shared with the representatives of that state. This will bring about the understanding of where there is common ground for all political persuasions. This information from a large number of the voters they represent, when shared with the representatives, will influence them to act. This will have impact as the information will be coming from a large number of their constituents. Currently, except for lobbyist groups, the representatives only get information from their voters in the form of individual contacts or small group petitioners. Due to lack of numbers these constituents get little attention and exceedingly small number of results. The Vote With Power movement will inform legislators of the wants and needs and recommendations from a majority of their constituents, which will have the influence.

You saw a pattern: Our journey will provide the short-term and eventually the long-term needed changes.

When is the last time you heard your representatives give long term plans with short term activities to make those plans come to fruition? Especially those which would fix our problems.

As we move forward and start to see success, the voters will begin to get excited and be involved in becoming part of America's future. We must *Vote with Power*.

Chapter 10

A New Path to Help Small Businesses Thrive

This chapter may seem odd to the reader. It does fit for the author as it represents a real need for our country. Strong, thriving small businesses are the stability and growth of our economy. Small businesses have the creativity and flexibility to keep our economy the best in the world, but only if we use tools to improve the success rate of new businesses. Our government attempts to help small businesses, but there are only a few programs that seem to help. This can be measured by the number of businesses that survive and do well in America.

Our federal government either needs to help small businesses or get out of the way. The data from the U.S. Bureau of Labor Statistics indicates that about 20 percent of small businesses fail within the first year. By the end of the fifth year almost 50 percent are gone. After ten years, only about one-third of the businesses have survived. Of those that survive, only about 7 percent of the 33 percent make it past survival level. Therefore, the business becomes a job and trap for the entrepreneur. For more information go to US Bureau of Labor Statistics and look up small business failure. This data supplied here came from www.lendingtree.com.

During these tough times, there are thousands of businesses closing forever.

There is hope. A new program started by the owner of Bar Stool Sports is helping small businesses. He is taking donations, which are now in the millions of dollars, and providing lifesaving money to small businesses all over our country. This is helping small businesses survive.

Bar Stools Sports has continued to grow and help more and more businesses facing difficult times. The uniqueness of this is that government, so far, has nothing to do with it. All Americans should help this cause, as this type of leadership will help sustain small businesses, which are the backbone of our economy.

We need to be creative with more and better ideas on how to greatly improve business success rates. As we do so, we need to keep government out of the way.

Small business owners are usually only skilled in their product or service and maybe one of the five critical areas of all businesses, which leaves them vulnerable in the other areas. If all entrepreneurs had training and skill development in Finance, Sales/Marketing, Human Resources, Leadership, and Operations, the success rate would go way up. Running a profitable small business is both art and science. It takes knowledge, skills, and d experience. One of the most important aspects is the skill to run a business. Most entrepreneurs only learn that skill through trial and error. This is time consuming, costly, and often the reason for a business to get stuck or fail.

In the following section, I have laid out a business helping plan that I wrote back in 2010.

We need to promote capitalism, so all Americans have the privilege, gain the knowledge, and develop the skills to run a profitable business. This will give citizens opportunities and a way to help others and will stabilize our economy. This could be a great advancement to change the low-income and underserved areas in our country.

Because of the way candidates fund their elections, they bend toward the big banks and big corporations and away from promoting and helping to develop entrepreneurs. They are allowing big tech to control our free speech and marketing methods. Congress has allowed big tech companies to become strong monopolies and buy out or crush their competition. Is that true capitalism? No! True capitalism is to let competition, if it is fair, run itself. Small businesses, due to their creativity and flexibility, are needed to fill niches to solve problems big business does not want to work on.

Small businesses also create most of the new products and services Americans enjoy. They provide vendors, customers, employees, and owners' families with a good lifestyle. They are the ones to increase employment opportunities and keep the unemployment numbers down.

Another way to look at the importance of small businesses to our economy is to see that our government is mostly funded by tax revenue. If small businesses did not have employees making a living, there would be a huge loss of tax revenue. Would your business survive if you did not pay attention to or service the people who brought in most of your business revenue?

We need to find out what Congress does to help small business and what Congress does to hinder small business success. From there we can eliminate some programs or regulations, modify others, and build programs to assist the success of all small businesses.

Our representatives need to understand where the money they spend mostly comes from: us taxpayers. Where do we get the money from? Working or owning a business.

I have always said if we want to add pressure to Congress to keep our income taxes fair, just change the law. Make all employees get their paycheck with the full amount of their gross wages, rather than have the employer deduct and collect and deposit the payroll taxes. When they must write a check to the federal government for the taxes due, the employee would not be happy with the amount. It would be in their focus. This would make them aware of the money they are giving up each paycheck. They would realize that a large part of their hard-earned money is going to the government. They would become more interested in and often offended by what Congress is doing with their money.

When their employers send the money to the government, the employee does not feel it. But they are still working to provide that money to our government. For now, most people do not know or are not sensitive to what they are giving to our government. The government needs the money to run our nation, but are they using it frugally and in the way we want them to use it? If voters were aware of the use of the money, it might have a great impact on the waste, pork, and money spent that the employee does not want spent. They would start to tell Congress that their tax dollars are for the American workers' lives, liberty, and the pursuit of happiness and not to be used as payback money for donations to get elected, for failing, or for ridiculous programs.

We need private for-profit small business development and funding centers with the responsibility to make sure the programs are well run and phenomenally successful.

Here is a unique economic system model and plans.

We can create a new type of economy, one that provides more jobs, a high level of small business success, continued economic growth, and stability!

The following is a new and different economic model that does not have a need for big businesses, big banks, or government influence or involvement. The small business development and funding centers' purpose and functions are to provide entrepreneurs with education and skill development in all five areas of running a small business profitably. The five areas of focus include Financial, Marketing/Sales, Operational, Human Resources, and Leadership. Each area would be delivered with an ongoing and in-depth training sequence to ensure success in all areas. Small business owners would become highly knowledgeable and skilled in running a small business. The centers will ensure all market research is conducted and provides accurate assessments before any small business loan is approved. This would ensure strong success rates. The center would also provide national information, referral sources, and networking opportunities from which owners could glean needed information. This would give them knowledge of resources such as the best practices and information from which to make good decisions based on their industry. The centers would find extraordinarily successful, knowledgeable, and skilled professionals to mentor, train, and coach entrepreneurs.

This strategy and organizations creating and supporting new businesses would make America the strongest nation in the world forever.

Following is my list of assumptions, which are supported by my many years in training and coaching hundreds of client small business owners and upper management. These are my assumptions:

1. The successful running of a small business is a learned behavior.
2. Small businesses can help create and grow a more stable economy; however, they need funding, education, training, skill development, and information.
3. There are millions and millions of dollars in money markets paying little interest.
4. Many Americans would invest in small business growth if they felt secure.
5. Funding and helping small business growth and development would create jobs.
6. Philanthropists could provide funds to back and insure small business loans for investor safety.
7. If small businesses had access to operating manuals, systems, and processes, skill development assistance, and other information as successful franchises do, their failure rates would be in the 3–5 percent range. Not 80 percent, like we have in nonfranchise start-ups.

Publicity and media about small business development centers could create positive attitudes and help Americans feel better about their future opportunities. With a way to start a business, with the comfort of knowing they would succeed if they got engaged with a center, with more people owning a small business, and a much lower failure rate, our economy would be stable and growing.

Stable small businesses will consistently create jobs as they grow, which will positively affect American families.

A strong economy based on small business success will also be beneficial to big businesses.

Small business loans from community members would need a new set of borrowing rules to ensure a 95 percent success rate.

These centers would have a great positive impact on inner-city, low-income areas. People who have not had the opportunity for advanced education can easily own a successful business. They need the centers to obtain the knowledge and skill development to run a profitable business. They would have the centers' ongoing support and training. This opens job opportunities in those poverty-stricken areas.

How will the small business development and funding centers work?

1. The center will only consider distributing any small business loans after the borrower has completed education and is connected to information networks to greatly lower their risk of failure. They will also be assigned a mentor to keep them on track.
2. Small business development and funding centers need to be directed by good supportive, caring leaders with small business experience, training skills, and expertise.
3. Every municipality in the United States could benefit from small business development and funding centers.
4. To be effective, the small business loans need to be offered with fair interest rates.
5. Small business development and funding centers would have private investing partners. This could be accomplished without government influence, oversight, or money.
6. This new economic structure could be implemented without the need for commercial bank funds.
7. The manager for each state office in our program will also need to be qualify by having small business background and a strong belief in the importance of small businesses in our economy.

8. Once the program is up and running, the money accumulated to start the program can be replaced from repayment of the centers' loans.

9. The program director needs to be a good speaker, trainer, and public figure, knowledgeable about the program design, human resources, and all phases of small business experience.

10. Once the economy is stabilized and continuously growing, the small business profitability would help fund future profit-sharing programs and health care for the employees.

11. Small businesses would add opportunities and financial security to our families, which in turn would create a stronger nation.

12. This strategy and economic model are creative and a new way of looking at supporting our economy.

13. Local middle-class families would greatly benefit from moving their money from low-paying CDs and money markets. If they received a safe 7 percent fixed rate return, they could accumulate needed assets to build their future income.

14. All loans granted to existing companies would be for the purpose of increasing revenue, profit, and job expansion. No loans would be granted as survival loans.

15. This new program would bring about more stable growth in jobs and incomes, which long-term could get young families in a better retirement position and soften the need for Social Security and Medicare in the future.

Plans for Implementing This New Type of Economy

This new approach can be utilized in every municipality that has the foresight and willingness to move their economy in a new and better direction. The plan is to have four sets of well-thought-out meetings, including one meeting for each of the following:

1. Local philanthropists for the investment safety funds.
2. Small business owners who might want to take part in the new developmental and funding centers.
3. Local families, to explain how the new model works and the benefits from investing in the centers to help local small businesses grow.
4. Once the new economic growth program is accepted by enough interested persons from the three groups, a director would be hired to work with the new leaders and staff to implement the plans.

Meetings would be scheduled, and the program would be off the ground. Media coverage and promotional opportunities would put the municipality in line for a successful installation process. Four winners would emerge: the small business owner, the American middle-class families, low-income inner-city citizens, and development centers of America. With enough municipalities successfully generating small business development and training, funding job creation would be prevalent as small businesses grow and become healthy and profitable.

This small business plan is not currently part of the journey or new organization, whose main purpose is to get our representatives to answer us, inform us, hear us, respect us, and represent us.

Chapter II

What Is Woke and How It Affects Our Lives

From the article "A Brief History of Wokeism," published in the online magazine *Open* (*openthemagazine.com*, June 2020) by Madhavankutty Pillai, I have a better understanding of wokeness, for which I thank the author. The definition of wokeness is to awaken against racism. The author further states that it has grown into an extreme ideology of justice. The justice in the definition is against all majority oppressions. The word "woke" started to be used frequently in social media platforms in 2014 after the death of Michael Brown in Ferguson, Missouri which sparked the Black Lives Matter movement. (according to independent.co,uk) Woke started as a slang term but has made its way into the mainstream. According to an article from *Merriam-Webster*, it comes from some varieties of African American Vernacular English and started as a term that meant, "I was sleeping, but now I'm woke!" Resource for this article is found in merriam-webster.com, titled "Words We're Watching Stay Woke."

It is being used to promote social awareness.

According to Merriam-Webster Dictionary, the phrase "stay woke" became a part of the black community and means "to be self-aware." In 2014, after the shooting of Michael Brown in Ferguson, Missouri, the phrase entered the media and became intertwined into the Black Lives Matter movement.

According to Lester Wong in the *Straits Times*, being woke, or socially conscious of injustice, is a good thing. But there is nothing gained from strong policing of other people's words and thoughts and any actions you judge as being improper. (www.straitstimes.com. Published January 10, 2021.

I have personally experienced the need for my wokeness. The situation is rare for a white middle-income, highly educated adult to experience. Right out of college, I went to work for Job Corps as a counselor. Job Corps was a government program to help young people who were having problems in society and getting an education. Most of the corpsmen came to our facilities from big inner-city areas. Many had faced a judge for minor crimes and had a choice of either going to Job Corps or prison. Their behavior had to be watched.

Often, they had "blanket parties." A group of corpsmen who did not like another corpsman would throw a blanket over the head of the person and beat them.

This group thug mentality was quickly imprinted on the counselors' minds. We became extremely sensitive to protecting the corpsmen and the possibility for personal danger. We learned to be woke to defend ourselves and stay out of the way of danger.

One counselor I knew was riding on a bus with corpsmen who were being taken into town for some free time. On the route back to the complex, the corpsman sitting behind the counselor grabbed the counselor's tie and pulled him back to choke him while a few corpsmen beat him.

That counselor had done nothing wrong except being in the wrong place at the wrong time with the wrong people. This to me was an example of woke behavior. This justified being the scapegoat for anger and injustice in the minds of the perpetrators. The formation of Job Corps was a great program. As all programs, it had some issues. It only takes a few bad apples to cast a blemish on the others.

My experience was a minor and short-term situation. However, it stayed with me for years after I left Job Corps, being extra sensitive to groups of males between the ages of seventeen and twenty-one. After I left Job Corps, I was and am still that way today, watching my surroundings to protect myself and family from danger. I am proud of the fact that I have only personally experienced racial discrimination twice in my life. Both were cases that it was me being discriminated against. The first was the Job Corps situation and the second was a hiring event. I applied to a large pharmaceutical manufacturing company. I was highly experienced, educated, and skilled in the human resources job opening qualifications. I received a call from a high-level management person from the department I was applying for. That person told me, which was probably illegal or at lease unethical, that I was the best candidate by far over any other candidate. I wasn't getting the job due to the affirmative action laws, and the person getting the job was a black female. That call gave me real-life experience in racism. I really wanted that job. Since there have been only two instances, I got over it quickly. I am sure people of any color who experience ongoing discrimination find it a major burden and not fair.

Black families use wokeness to educate their children on being aware and sensitive to not only police brutality but to never put yourself in the way of danger from other people and injustice of any form.

These threats and fear should not have to be part of our American culture. We need to stop the violence against any race, religion, nationality, class, creed, or color. To eradicate this violent behavior, we must harshly deal with those who live a different lifestyle than the honest caring citizens of America.

Wokeness has transformed and grown into the accepted meaning of all perceived social injustice. The question is what the facts are and who gets to decide what social injustice is.

Woke is no longer a word that points out awareness of injustice or racial tension; it has become a word of action. This verb has the potential for major destruction to our citizens, businesses, and our country.

Where we go from here is very threatening to our culture and democracy. Now social media is taking away the right of free speech, to a point of killing businesses, job opportunities, and the livelihood of Americans who do not have the same political beliefs as those in power.

This must be stopped. It is dividing our nation. It will enforce and strengthen the political divide. Twitter is now stopping whoever they want from using their platform. This use of power and actions are supported by Apple, Amazon, and Google. Where do those who do not align with their political beliefs go?

Now we are faced with white fragility training. This concept is destructive and creating new racism. If not stopped, it will eventually cause America to return to hate and segregation. The training has a purpose for creating shame in all white people due to our history of bad treatment and slavery of black people. According to the article in the Atlantic written by John

McWhorter on July 15, 2020, the concept is to combat racism but actually talks down to black people. (theatlantic.com). The training is presented an antiracism effort. There are white people who want to be equal to all races. Another group of white people are led to a high level of guilt because they are white, maybe because their ancestors hundreds of years ago had slaves. We are starting to see political and left-right segregation? This time it will not be racial, it will be judgmental, based on opinions. Will we have left and right restaurants, drinking fountains, seats on the bus, and designated bathrooms we can use? This will become high-powered destructive segregation all over again. Big business is deciding what to sell based on the political philosophies of the owners of the businesses they buy from. Will you choose what restaurants to go to by political opinions?

Activists were waking up and wanted others to stay woke.

The word "woke" has also morphed into an adjective. It represents places where woke people commune, such as woke Twitter.

The word "woke" entered the Oxford English Dictionary in 2017, as explained in the *Guardian*. The Guardian is a Manhattan-based American online presence of the British print newspaper. It launched in September 2011 and can be found at theguardian.com.

If you want more history on wokeness, go to VOX and their article, "What Is Woke: How a Black Movement Watchword Got Co-opted in a Cultural War." Vox is an American website owned by Vox Media founded in April 2014 by Ezra Klein, Matt Yglesias, and Melissa Bell it is noted for its concept of explanatory journalism.

A question for us voters: Is this a concept only? Or is it a call to action from activists that must be watched and forced to stay within our laws that protect us?

For those reading this book who are for a united nation of freedom and opportunities for all Americans, this is your woke call. Now we need to be woke to protect us from big money, lobbyists, tech companies, and the political parties. They all want the power. Voters cannot continue to give our power to any of them.

We must be heard, answered, respected, informed, and represented.

If you agree and want to be part of this movement, please go to www.votewithpower.com.

The American public must become extremely *woke* on the government's position of ignoring cancel culture. This trend is driving us away from our freedoms, safety, and our Constitution.

Chapter 12

What Is Cancel Culture and How Will It Ruin Your Lifestyle?

Wikipedia defines cancel culture (or call-out culture) as today's form of ostracism. It is criticism and attempts to throw someone out of social or professional circles. It is frequently found online or in social media. It has expanded into our schools. One school system is attempting to stop their students from using the words "mom," "dad," "sister," or "brother." In an article found in USA Today with the title NYC schools defend inclusive language guide asking students, parents to avoid phrases like "mom and dad" Written by Dustin Barnes March 12, 2021. In the article it refers to Grace Church School asking for its community to replace the use of "Mom and Dad" with grown-ups, folks, or family. To use the word "people", instead of boys and girls. One example can be found in an article in the *New York Post* by Elizabeth Elizalde on March 10, 2021, titled, "NYC Schools encourage kids to stop using the words like Mom and Dad in inclusion language guide." There are many articles on school policies calling for gender-neutral language to be used. The word suggested to replace "mom" is "my birthing person." A good source of information on this subject is on the website found on google breezy.hr or University of Wisconsin – Milwaukee (uwm.edu/lgbtrc/support. Even the White House changed. An article written on January 21, 2021, in Reuters Mx on the White House websites' contact page, which also added a drop – down list of personal pronouns, including "they/them".

According to *Wikipedia* the definition of cancel culture refers to the popular practice of canceling or removing support of people and companies after they have said or done what the shamers feel is objectionable.

It is a method of group shaming of anyone or any organization you perceive as objectionable in your thoughts and behaviors. This is strictly opinion-based and highly emotional.

According to an article in the New York Post written by Brooke Kato on March 10, 2021, cancel culture – the phenomenon of promoting the "canceling" of people, brands and even shows and movies due to what some consider to be offensive or problematic remarks or ideologies.

It is not a real cultural strategy. The culture change movement is attempting to destroy statues, movies, art, and music. Targeted Disney moves are *Dumbo, Peter Pan*, and *Swiss Family Robinson*, according to the Focus News. Focus news is the official paper of record for DeSoto, Duncanville, Cedar Hill, Lancaster and Glenn Heights, Texas. (focusnews.com). According to Theurbanlist artist who stated, "We have seen it with Gwen Stefani, Ja Rle, Iggy Azalea, Taylor Swift, R. Kelly and Michael Jackson back in the year of 2019. In St. Paul Minnesota, the statue of Columbus came down according to the New York Times. Article written by Johnny Diaz, published June 10, 2020.

Those people who are attempting to destroy our past, don't like our culture, they are trying to remove anything they feel does not represent their beliefs. Their mission is to remove America's history.

If a statue of a historically important figure had a slave way back in the 1800s, that statue, no matter what that person contributed to America, in their views, should be torn down.

We need our history. We learn the good and bad from what our history represents. We build on our successes and refrain from repeating or perpetuating the dark parts of our history. We do not have to relive the bad past, but we do need to remember what we have been through, the good and bad. Our history is where we came from.

If your children ask about their grandparents, should you just say, "They were not important, they made some bad choices and mistakes; so let's not talk about them"? Or do you want to preserve and honor your heritage? The good and bad is still our history. We need to learn from it.

Where will this stop? Do we not allow for any history to be experienced or recorded?

Rob Henderson received his BS degree in psychology from Yale University and is a veteran of the US Air Force. In his article, "Five Reasons Why People Love Cancel Culture," in *Psychology Today* (December 1, 2019), written when he was a PhD student at the University of Cambridge, he defines cancel culture as the activities of a large group of people, usually on social media outlets, target people who in their mind have violated their moral code. Any code they believe in.

The eight reasons Henderson lists are as follows.

1. Cancel culture increases social status. This culture is to give advocates new opportunities for social gain, who need to either move up themselves or take others down.

2. Cancel culture reduces the social status of enemies.

3. There are two ways to gain status. One can do something of value, but that takes work, time, and has risks. The other way is to demean others, often done through grandstanding. If someone lowers the social status level of someone, that in their minds moves them up on their own social level.

4. Cancel culture strengthens social bonds.

5. The article stated that people unite to gain group solidarity. They will join each other in demeaning their target. They will not try to do something good due to the possibility of failure. When they take action to destroy someone, even if they do not totally accomplish that goal, they still have feelings of power from socially bonding with members of the group. Their attempts at canceling someone, even when they are not successful, provides opportunities to get recognition and build themselves a higher social status.

6. Cancel culture forces enemies to reveal themselves. It is all created by false judgment.

7. This helps them identify others who have loyalty to the same movement. Many of the actions of these groups are aimed at targets that have done something that has gone out of fashion. It is easy to grow your group around morally ambiguous bad behavior and watch the reactions; this helps in recruiting other dissenters to help attack a defined target.

8. Cancel culture produces fast rewards.

The social rewards of higher status and belonging to the group provides immediate gratification. These benefits to me sound like the reasons gangs have "family" members.

Cancel culture is gotten out of hand. TV shows, journalists, musicians, magazine writers, and anyone who has a Twitter, Facebook, or Instagram account can be canceled. This is happening every day and done quickly, without rational thoughts behind the cancellation. Canceling has expanded to deeper levels of putting employees out of work or closing businesses. Even retail stores are deciding to only sell the wares of the suppliers based on their political views.

This means that political correctness is becoming a predominant factor in decisions such as who you should hire, which social media platforms you can be on, who should be fired. The article in Forbes (forbes.com) written by Evan Gerstman published on September 13, 2020, list many examples of people being fired due to cancel culture experiences.

There have been attempts to use cancel culture to remove hard earned college degrees. The article in Harvard University students signed a petition to have Harvard remove the degrees earned by some individuals. In a Fox Business article "Harvard students seek to revoke Donald Trump's diploma after the Capital Hill violence, written January 14, 2021, by Lydia Moynihan, explains students at Harvard University sought to revoke the diplomas of graduates who supported Donald Trump, after the Capitol Hill violence. (foxbusiness.com)

I have said for months that the emotionally charged prejudices and self-advancement of cancel culture advocates' definition of social justice is dividing our country. We are heading toward two separate cultures and classes of businesses, including restaurants, and violent social mores. It has become all right to attack anyone your group does not like, for any reason.

Instead of caring about, understanding, helping, and respecting each other, our culture has changed into a bullying, attention-getting type of culture. Many people spend their time downplaying other people, instead of the morally correct behavior of helping others. This is the attitude of being against others having self-confidence, self-awareness, and self-worth. The person who belittles others is coming from a point of jealousy. If they bash you, that in their minds brings you down and raises them to a higher value in our society. This never really brings the person up and is a terrible way to live for both the basher and the person being bashed.

My question for those pushing to cancel our culture is what do they advocate we replace it with? There will always be a culture, but will it be a different culture for every citizen? We need a national culture based on our core values. No one has the right to change the core values and culture of America.

I have two new words to be added to the dictionaries, when it comes to cancel culture. Are you a "cancelee" or "cancellor"? Which side of that coin do we want our citizens to be on? Let us tell our representatives it is time to stop this insanity. Those folks doing the canceling, who hate America, should, in my opinion, move to another country.

Even a lion's pride has a culture. A pecking order of power, which determines, for instance, who gets the food first and where they move and sleep. There is a communication system based on size, strength, and gender. They have their own pride makeup and class system. They have their own survival core values and duties.

If we allow those who hate America to cancel our culture, what will our country's values be? Should we alter our values, or mores? Do we change our need for safety, job opportunity, and family structure as prescribed by those who want to cancel our lifestyles? Will we become a society based on survival and freedom of those who are the fittest? Part of our definition of the fittest is those who have the most money and power. We lovers of our country need to *Vote with Power!*

People with high levels of self-confidence are not disrupted as much be this canceling behavior. They will pay less attention. This will only change if the masses around them add to the bashing. It has grown from name-calling to public degrading and to attempt to destroy anyone you disagree with.

Cancel culture, if left to expand, will be in your neighborhood soon. You could be next! Unless you join our journey to get our representatives making American citizens first over those who want to change our culture.

Antifa is threatening individuals they do not agree with by means of Facebook and Twitter. The radio host, Jason Rantz was standing in the middle of one of the Antifa riots was giving his story of what was really happening. A news cast written by Joshua Q Nelson on Fox News titled Rantz rips media for reporting on Portland violence: "would be laughable if it wasn't so serious. Rantz was a guest on the "The Faulkner Focus" a tv show on Fox, to explain what happened to him after his news cast. There were posts with his picture, threats, and calling for people to cancel him are negatively affecting his life and livelihood. They are also using social media to advertise their next place of crusade (riot) so they can have more people join them to bust windows and destroy businesses.

If you want to see the impact of these behaviors on other countries, look at East Germany under Honecker and China under Mao.

This movement is a social class restructuring. If allowed to continue, it will destroy our country.

Let us look at China's history and their Cultural Revolution.

In the article in Wikipedia called "Cultural Revolution, (en.m.wikipedia.org)we can gain some insights as to what happened in China.

According to the article, the cultural revolution group started a movement in May of 1966. It was a social political movement for the purpose of preserving Chinese communism by purging what was left from their capitalism and traditional parts of Chinese society. It was organized and promoted by Mao Zedong, chairman of the Communist Party of China at that time.

He launched the movement by calling on young people to attack the headquarters in China and declared that to rebel is justified.

This became a violent class struggle. The youths on one side and the bourgeois on the other. Mao felt the upper social class was infiltrating the government and society with plans for restoring capitalism.

The next few years in China saw many political leaders change positions and authority. This was a revolution that destroyed China's economy and traditional culture. They experienced an estimated death toll as high as 20 million, due to the revolution. The lack of a more accurate estimate is likely due to the lack of transparency of Mao's regime and the difficulty in obtaining reliable historical records.

Mao launched a social education movement—the purpose was to get rid of powerful officials who had questionable loyalty to the current power of Mao.

The national police chief, Xie Fuzhi, often pardoned Red Guard members for their crimes.

The great proletarian cultural revolution was later called the Sixteen Points. The decision to go that way was to create, according to the quote from Mao, a "great revolution that touches people to their very souls and constitutes a deeper and more extensive stage in the development of the socialist revolution in our country."

The intent was to elevate the student movement to a nationwide campaign that would bring together workers, farmers, soldiers, and lower-level party staff to rise up and challenge authority and reshape the superstructure of Chinese society.

The Red Guard was a group of representatives of the rebellion attempting to direct the future of China through violence and upheaval. They were the force behind Mao.

In August 1966 there was a central directive to stop police intervention in Red Guard activities. The police who defied that directive were held out as counterrevolutionaries.

If you follow the years after Mao died, you will find how China became a Communist Party oligarchy. Then it shifted to a dictatorship, one that is trying to control the world.

Think about America's current situation. The cancel culture here at home is creating civil unrest, defund the police movements, and racist thought in every aspect of our lives.

Therefore, we need to use our "vote with power" organization to direct Congress in the best interests of the American voters. Cancel culture must be reduced and eventually eliminated.

Some of our municipalities' power structures are hindering their police and other protection officers from stopping violent behavior. We have sanctuary cities that protect criminals from being arrested. They are becoming lawless. The only way we the American people can do something about it is to take back our power through representation. We need to change the mindsets or eliminate those leaders who protect the dissenters.

Cancel culture is destroying small businesses. Small business is the stability and sustained growth of our economy. Once the voters get back in power, we need to put small business in the forefront of our focused efforts to help them.

We must *Vote with Power* to save our country and protect the core values of most Americans. Which America do you want to live in? Keep improving what we have or let the radicals cancel our culture?

Chapter 13

Gerrymandering: Its Purpose and Influence

According to Merriam-Webster, (abridged. meriam-webster.com) the term for dividing or arranging a territorial unit into election districts in a way that gives one political party an unfair advantage in elections is called "gerrymandering." It is the process whereby politicians use their power to redraw lines in their political party's favor, for the purpose of getting more votes.

The basis for gerrymandering comes from the census results. It is used to allocate seats in Congress and for the distribution of government funding for essential services. The practice of gerrymandering is not applied consistently or fairly! It is a political tool used by both parties.

Many consider the gerrymandering process to be promoting voter suppression. It does limit voter rights. We do not have the right to elect the representative based on how we want them to function in their job. Every ten years the states redraw electoral districts. This has important consequences. If it were a fair and just process, it would represent the will of the voters.

Those who get to draw the lines on the map can pack and break up the population to make votes count in the direction they want. This gives them unearned and unfair power.

We the voters must change the system to represent voters' expectations and desires. Stop the political influence that allows one party an unfair advantage over the other to get extra votes and direct our nation.

We must get fired up about reform.

In the report written on July 8, 2020, for the Center for American Progress, Alex Tausanovitch and Danielle Root described the following. (I am paraphrasing and focusing on the points that are most relevant for our discussion.) In the last election 2018. The authors' assessment was that due to gerrymandering in four states. North Carolina, Michigan, Pennsylvania, and Wisconsin democracy did not happen. (americanprogress. org) This article was Titled "How Partisan Gerrymandering Limits Voting Rights.

To make this situation worse, gerrymandering, the way it is used, places restrictions on voter freedom in each of those states. These practices are used by both political parties. They are both guilty.

The big issue is that representatives did not get the votes but gained the power to make it harder for citizens to vote, which drives a wedge in voters' ability to hold Congress accountable.

The article went on to say that we need to empower an independent commission to draw voter-led districts that will reflect the will of the people.

Here is another example of how politics is all about helping their friends and hurting their enemies. We need to wake up and use a system that provides transparency, accountability, and places responsibility on our elected representatives. We need to stop the political war.

Totally changing the rules for redistricting will be almost impossible, but we can certainly clean the process up.

Redistricting takes place every ten years in forty-three states. There are currently seven states with only one house representative, that due to low population, do not have to redistrict (according to Wikipedia). Thirty-three states must redistrict every ten years by law. This is to take into account shifts in populations.

This gerrymandering practice, if not altered, will change our representation dramatically. The political use of voter packing by gerrymandering is mostly hidden within the politicians agenda. This process will change as our citizens move from one state to another and change the states demographics in our future. Especially as gerrymandering only takes place every ten years. These population shifts will drastically change our demographics and our voting populations.

Chapter 14

A Model for a Better Government

If we are to keep our democratic system, the voters need to be the leading class, not our political elite. Our power should not be based on how we look, our color, our religion, or our wealth. The voters need to be heard, answered, informed, respected, and represented.

We need to set up a transparency and accountability communication loop office in each state, to open dialogue with each senator and each representative. This is the only way to educate, trade information, get answers, provide input, and rate the representatives' performance and voting records.

The new process must ensure our representatives know where their constituents stand on the relevant issues. The major issues need to be understood and have input from the constituents before our representatives vote.

These centers will not take a political position, be judgmental or political, share information that is biased, or try to become influencers. This is the privilege and duty of the voters. The centers' job is to be neutral, to collect constituent ideas and wishes, and be a conduit to help Congress know and represent the voters. We will also stay in touch with Congress to get their opinions and reasons for voting the way they do. This will be a great source for information the public wants or needs to know. No more partial truths or hidden agendas.

Our centers cannot become a left or right influencing lobbyist group. The centers need to communicate the Truth through transparency from a large number of voters.

Congress has been full of hypocrisy and enjoys their double standards. We the voters cannot allow that behavior to continue. We need to push back through a focused effort to force change.

On February 9, 2021, the news, (cnn.com), CNN Politics live TV titled Trump's second impeachment trial: day 1 was talking about the House and Senate representatives who would most likely vote to impeach the president. The president was seven days away from leaving the White House. He would be out of office before the impeachment process could be completed. It does not matter which side of the impeachment trial you believe in. We all need to be somewhat flexible to get along. We must be informed and go along the facts, process, and what is right. Did Congress on either side inform you of the entire truth or ask for your input? No. What do we lack when decisions on either side do not fit with the wishes of a majority of the voters in the state? Without voter input, the solutions are political solutions and do not represent the voters. We lack representation. Do you feel representatives are oversensitive about their job security? I do. That is why they spend most of their time and networking on getting reelected. This controls their focus, their purpose for existence, and takes most of their time.

We voters should have huge concerns for the voting process. It appears that members of one party will most likely vote based on their being a party puppet. The other side of the aisle, in the Senate, seems slightly less party directed and told to vote as they wish. Both sides are always posturing to see how their vote will affect their next election. Members need to learn to listen to their constituents and vote the right way by representing their voters.

Here are the problems I see. We voters always take a back seat to other factions. Our elected officials spend many votes along party lines. However, they are spending all their efforts finding out how to position themselves and voting for one reason: How do I get reelected? Instead of voting for what is right and important to United States citizens.

Much time and effort are spent by members of Congress to silence and even cancel the concerns and views of the voters. Do we want them to do our bidding or allow them to vote on behalf of their donors? There should be consequences when they do not vote the way we want them to vote. Those who vote in the interest of other influencers need to be voted out of office.

The journey and center organizations I am proposing through this book will be more effective, faster, and longer lasting than trying to pass term limits. Once they are implemented and adhered to, our representatives will be forced to hear us, answer us, inform us, respect us, and represent us. Once that is accomplished, our representatives will find this organization and process highly valuable to them. Term limits will be on autopilot as voters will vote out the nonconforming elected officials who fail to represent the voters.

The design of this journey has a way for thousands of voters to respond to polls, surveys, and questionnaires. Input from those who have joined the Vote With Power movement will provide the representatives with honest, statistically correct representative ideas, positions on bills, and their desired improvements in our country.

A new system will be run by the state centers to give the voters the performance and voting records of those who represent them, including what percent of the time they voted, how often they voted along party lines, and how they are staying in touch with their constituents before voting. This is the fastest and best way to get our representatives' attention and break the current power structure.

The representative will have access to information from thousands of voters. Through polls, surveys, and questionnaires, they will have all the statistically measured results to have enough voter input to know how to best represent their voters.

Members of Congress know from the voters' perspective what is right, legal, important, and how we want our Constitution followed. We must help keep our nation strong and resilient through the efforts and convictions of most voters with the help of Congress. It is not just Congress' job but partly our responsibility to guide them. Newly elected representatives in Congress quickly learn the ropes of voting for their party and the people who paid for their election.

Another issue, once we regain our vote with power, is to direct the focus and what our representatives are working on. The citizens have problems they need solved and ideas that may help America. Most legislation today and items for conflict resolution come from big donors, states, and other large organizations. They have size and power to influence Congress and have Congress work to resolve their problems. The individual voter has almost no chance of getting attention. Through the centers I am proposing, each voter will be heard. Then there will be research and analysis to find out if this is a one-person issue or there are many separate individuals with the same idea or concern. If it is a single concern, the center will find a resource and refer the person to that entity. If it is more widespread, then it will be passed on to the representative, and a response will be requested.

A few of the huge concerns that we are facing are getting the vaccine out, lowering our national debt, overcoming the cyberattacks on our technology and infrastructure from foreign countries, and threats from China, Russia, North Korea, and Iran.

In July of 2015 in one of the sanctuary cites, an illegal alien killed a young lady. He had been deported ten times from America for criminal activities in the past. What about the number of murders in large cities? Or the inner-city low-income people who need real help? We need representatives who will stop playing politics and work on solutions.

What is Congress doing to help the small business owners survive the effects and government mandates of closure caused by COVID-19?

We deserve answers to what Congress is doing to alleviate these problems. Do you think our representatives are doing their job and solving these concerns? Or are they wasting time focusing on issues for political purposes? Businesses need metrics and measurables. To be profitable and grow, businesses need to have and use comparisons. In business we use comparisons of that businesses historical results, against that businesses goals, and against the competition.

They set smart goals and track and measure them against their progress. They also set up processes and systems and measure planned activities in relationship to completed tasks to accomplish behavioral changes.

To improve our government's approaches and the way they operate, they need to make the following changes, in addition to being transparent and accountable.

In the business parts of our government, they should set goals from the following questions and measurement tools.

1. How often and by what percent will they stay within their budget?

2. What is their goal, in dollars, and timeline for paying off debt?

3. How much is their goal for increasing the living standard of Americans? In percent.

4. How many people do they want raised out of poverty? In numbers.

5. How much do they want to reduce the crime rate? In percent.

6. What is their goal for the reducing the level of unemployment? By percent.

7. How many people will they get out of poverty? By numbers.

8. What is the goal for the gross national product? In dollars.

9. How much will we decrease drug abuse deaths? In numbers and percent.

I could list more, but you get the idea. Our politicians will claim they have zero impact on these growth changes. No matter how loudly they kick and scream, we will not back off. Voter power through performance and voting records holds the key to their reelection.

In business, you need to measure your results and work completed against three criteria. First, against your goals; second, against your historic data; and third, against your competition. In this case, how are we doing in the major concern areas against China?

Congress needs direction to work from a mission, goals, and plans to be purposeful on behalf of their constituents. Their efforts need to be tracked and the results shared with their voters.

What if we could get our representatives' attention and ask what each of them has done for America or "we the voters" in the last year? What do you think the answers would be?

A major concern to me is that we do not vet our elected officials before we vote for them. We need to know what experiences, education, accomplishments, and results they have gotten in the past, in addition to how they think and what are their core values. We often vote along party lines.

We need to stop supporting those who get on national TV and social media and only disrespect and blame others in Congress for everything that is not right in their minds.

We need to stop buying into the negative, slanted opinions and judgments. We want our representatives to tell us what they are accomplishing for us. Voters deserve the whole truth. Our members of Congress need, though they will not like it at first, to know how the voters feel they are doing their jobs. Our representatives get high grades by voting along party lines. Their grades are much different when voters rate them. The journey will provide the tools for voters to rate our representatives. This will alter the motivation for voting along party lines.

The centers will have a six-month job performance review for each representative in their state.

What would the voters' ratings be if we filled out a performance review of our leaders over the past year? How would our Congress members be rated on being honest with us? How would they be rated on their job accomplishments, on listening to us, answering us, giving information to us, respecting us, and representing us? I am certain for most representatives their ratings would be low.

Most voters see our representatives as arrogant, self-serving, or do-nothing and lazy. They may be proud of themselves for what they did for their party and influencers. To do their job, our representatives need a real picture of how they are representing the voters from the voters' point of view. Their performance review will supply this information.

The way for the elected officials to gain a high level of appreciation and respect from us is to become transparent and accountable and work with us on *our* aspirations, not the goals of their party and big money.

From there, they will have the gratitude of the people they represent and work for. Where else can they get job fulfillment? We will give recognition for what and how they served us, but only if they earned it!

This will help our representatives fulfill their need for hearing us, answering us, informing us, respecting us, and representing us.

Set these communication loop centers up with funds from the membership of individual American citizens. A small monthly fee will be charged to frequently poll their opinions and give them the reasons behind the voting records of their representatives. This will alter the way our government functions.

This communication system will also focus on one-issue bills, so the representatives and public will be able to know what is in the bill, what the funds will be allocated to, why our representative is or is not for it, and what their constituents want from it.

No more thousands of pages of multiple-issue bills that are full of pork trade-offs. How can anyone vote for what they have not read and understand or will be held responsible for?

Our legislators need to do the following:

Operate from a budget.

Stop using pork to get the bills passed.

Start building common ground with their voters for the purpose of representing the people over all others.

Stop blaming and attacking other members of Congress to make their point and get their party's votes.

Stop running on tearing down their competitors to win an election. They need ideas and clarity of what and how they will advance the lifestyles of their constituents, not blaming or selling fear or false hope.

Start running on ideas with measurable results. Evaluate their results against their goals to track success. Run on actual plans. Tell the voters how they are going to help all Americans. They will have access to good jobs, higher income, less neighborhood crime, and work to avoid wars, help schools get great results, and lower national debt (by what percent?).

They will no longer just sell us empty words. We will only accept workable plans. Candidates have sold us too many times on the theme, "I will make things better; your life will be great." In business when managers have ideas to make improvements, they must use smart goals, express expected results, offer plans, and tell the truth of any downside effects they anticipate.

Our representatives do not look at government as a business. Starting now, they need to. Or they must leave.

We need a nonpolitical advisory board to keep a check on the growing bureaucracies and make sure all new regulations are in the interests of the people. Stop trying to overprotect us.

A good example is during 1982 the big banks lobbied and got legislation named the Garn-St. Germain Depository Institutions Act passed. This created the "due-on-sale clause" in all federally backed home mortgages. This hurt the American people's flexibility to sell their homes. Its purpose for the banks was to make loans paid off if you sold your home. Anyone with a mortgage who sold their home were forced to pay off the mortgage. This eradicated other options to sell a home. From my point of view, the banks were more secure if there were land contracts stacked on top of the person who took out the mortgage. Bank safety would be enhanced due to having more people in line who had a contract to pay off or lose their equity.

Instead of having one interested and responsible family to pay back the loan, they now had as many people as possible who would lose if the mortgage payments were not made. The real reason for banks lobbying was to get their money back upon the sales of the home so they could loan it out again, especially if the interest rates were higher. Another reason banks wanted this law was because the first few years of a mortgage, payments mainly go toward interest. After a few years, much of the payment goes to the principal. The banks were happy when people had to pay off their mortgage about halfway through the amortization schedule. At that point, the bank would loan it out again and get mostly interest.

A few years after that occurred, the big banks lobbyists went after land contract sales. That legislation passed. An investor could no longer buy homes and sell more than one or two per year on land contracts. This applied to all homes, not just the ones with bank mortgages on them. This hurts the investors and the public but helps the banks. People could buy a home on land contract with less down payment and with a lower credit score than the banks require. This forced the use of more mortgages. The bank wins, and the representatives get more big donations.

It protects the banks by forcing people to get a mortgage and reduces the banks' competition.

Where was Congress focused as they passed these bills? Was it in the best interests of the American people? No!

Did this new law help or hurt the citizens? It made it more difficult to sell their homes. Without alternative financing from land contracts, the banks become the only game in town. To stop Congress from supporting big money and not caring about the voters, it is time for change. We must *Vote with Power.*

Chapter 15

Equality vs Equity,

From an article written by Daisy Veerasingham of the Associated Press, on March 29, 2019, the definition of "equality" is to ensure that every individual has equal opportunities to make the most out of their lives.

In addition to having the same opportunities, individuals must have the same support and treatment.

To offer similar opportunities, support may be on different levels. For instance, students who are disadvantaged need more support to get them to their full potential.

Daisy provides the opinion that our society strives for equality, but it is not that easy. Some individuals need different and often more treatment and support than others.

The article goes on to explain the definition for equity. It is defined as giving people what they need for them to enjoy fairness. This means giving more to people who need it. This term, "equity," is not the same as equality or inequity.

This article goes into contrasting equality and equity in this way. Both promote fairness, but equality gets the results through having the same treatment for all, while equity achieves the results by treating people differently. Equity maybe the catalyst that can help reach equality.

Some see the goal being equality, and the path to get there is through equity.

Another way to state this contrast is explained in a blog by the Annie E. Casey Foundation, (aecf.org) "Equity vs Equality and other Racial Justice Definitions" (August 24, 2020).

This article compares both concepts: equity involves understanding and giving individuals what they need to enjoy a fulfilling and healthy life, while equality, in contrast, aims to make sure everyone gets the same thing to have a healthy and fulfilling life.

A recent $1.9 trillion spending bill provides huge amounts of grant money to black farmers. Congress sees this as equity. How does this meet the equality test? If you look at it closely, it sounds like promoting racism. I will let you decide.

From the "Executive Order on Advancing Racial Equity and Support for Underserved Communities Through the Federal Government," our current president, Joe Biden, signed an executive order on January 20 of 2021 that contained in part of the policy the following paragraph, and I quote: "Entrenched disparities in our laws and public policies, and in our public and private institutions, have denied equal opportunity to individuals and communities. Our country faced converging economic, health and climate crises that have exposed the unbearable human costs of systemic racism." (whitehouse.gov presidential actions.)

The definitions for this executive order are as follows: "The term 'equity' means the consistent and systematic fair, just and impartial treatment of all individuals, including individuals who belong to underserved communities that have been denied such treatment, such as blacks, Latino, and Indigenous and Native

American persons, Asian, American Pacific Islanders and other persons of color; members of religious minorities; lesbian, bisexual, transgender, and queer (LGBTQ+) persons; persons with disabilities, persons who live in rural areas; and persons adversely affected by persistent poverty or inequality.'"

An article written in the NEA (National Education Association) web page thoughts about race based in history, organizations, and culture. According to the article there are routinely advantages for white people and disadvantages to people of color. Find more information in edjustice (neajustice,org). Back issue titled "Racial Justice is Educations Justice."

The article went on to say that some racism is conscious and intentional; however, much of racism is unconscious and unintentional. Racism can be magnified when interacting with other inequities such as gender and class.

These two core concepts, equity, and equality are being played out in our government. They are infiltrating our educational organizations, institutions, and communities. They are not being looked at from a fair, just, responsible, and accountability management point of view.

A good example of Congress creating a negative equity proposal is the current interest in paying off student loans up to $50,000 for each student. How is this equity? What is the reaction of and fairness to those who have struggled over the past few years to pay off their college debts?

It is also important to get ideas and opinions on how to approach our problems in these areas. If you listen to the people who want to help minorities and poverty-stricken communities, they have one approach, and if you listen to and read articles from Bob Woodson's organization, Woodson Center, (woodsoncenter. org), you will find a different approach. For another opinion on the cause of today's inequity problems, read Shelby Steele's book,

Shame, America's Past Sins Have Polarized Our Country. You also should read Candace Owens, book, *Blackout.* We need to stop name-calling and create programs to further stop racism. Many of these programs actually promote racism. This will not be easy, but where is name-calling getting us now? We need more than one approach be blended for a faster and more fair transition. Or do we do most things in an American style, where our egos get involved and we want our way and only our way?

One of the most volatile ideas in our nation is the concept of reparation. This is an attempt to get Congress to make amends to all black people in America, to make a large payout to each Black individual to have equity. This came about because their ancestors, many years ago, were slaves. Many Americans, even many Black people, disagree. They see that this money is not warranted or that it won't do any good. My concern is that this going to create more hate and racism? It you think about it, this program is racist in it's purpose.

We have to do more and better to eradicate racism. We need action, no more talk, except for dialogue on how to solve these problems. Our "vote with power" journey will open communication, understanding, and a planning process to improve our situation. Congress only uses one solution. That is to throw money at problems. This never solves anything.

Chapter 16

Our New Journey Together

I have designed an approach to hold our politicians accountable and force transparency. We voters need to understand what is in every important and major bill before it is voted on by our elected officials. The voters need a way to communicate their preferences to their representatives. The voters want answers to why our representatives voted and fought for issues that were not in line with what their constituents wanted.

Our new journey must be organized, planned out, well communicated, heavily marketed, and put into action. This book will lay out the foundation, procedure, and organizational plan for our journey. Through this we can build the needed two-way communication system. This plan, once implemented, will be extraordinarily successful once voters' level of interest and involvement is high enough. It is the only way to improve our government's representation of the voters.

The task of the state communication loop offices will be to develop and sustain a two-way communication system, which will create dialogue between the voters of that state and their representatives. It will provide ongoing trade of ideas and interest of both voters and their representatives. The office director and staff will send out or email surveys and questionnaires and conduct or oversee polling activities. They also may use focus groups when appropriate. The office staff will have a system for analyzing the results and putting them into a report. The report will be immediately given to both the voters and their representatives. This will give our representatives accurate information from which to make better voter focused decisions.

Another duty of the state office will be to promote membership. The more voters who are involved, the higher the level of accuracy and the more comprehensive information the representatives will get from the voters.

The state offices will also track the performance, accomplishments, and voting records of their legislators. They will write a review to be shared with the voters and the representatives. The report card will be categorized to tell how they vote, how often they voted, and how often they voted in alignment with the voter input. What percent of their votes were along party lines? What percent of the total votes available to vote on did they actually vote? In addition, part of the report will give a performance review analysis.

Through utilization of performance and voting reviews, the voters will increase representatives' transparency. Voters need to start knowing what their representatives are doing and accomplishing and how they vote. From that point the voters can regain their power and attention from their representatives and keep their freedom of speech. Next, voters will be able to direct their representatives along the path the voters want. This will have a huge impact on turning our government and country around.

We must never forget our representatives work for us, not the other way around. Nor are we, the taxpayers, the representatives' source of money, which they spend and waste on anything they want.

The state offices will be headquartered by one national office. The purpose of the national office is to do research on each national bill to get all the salient information. Without prejudice, the national office will also hire companies that will prepare the survey and poll questions. This method will provide high-quality information-gathering methods that will be as accurate as possible.

A current example of how an approach like this is working can be found in the news. A united citizens group was collecting signatures to impeach and remove California Governor Gavin Newsom from office. The general public, at least two million of them, do not like his decisions, demeanor, hypocritical behaviors, and feels he fails to represent the voters. They have close to two million signatures.

The point I want to make is that there are two million dissatisfied citizens who are not only upset, but they are also taking action due to his performance and lack of representation. The two million are made up of both parties, liberals, and conservatives, including minorities and different races and religions. They have come together to make changes in their state government. This is a sign that the journey in this book can and will come true, with your help!

Even though the citizens' efforts to remove the governor are just starting at the time of this writing, the important point is that people are standing up and agreeing to come together and are doing something to make desired changes. Most Americans are fed up with our government. This journey adds a new perspective. It provides a source to do something.

The current process of creating bills that contain many completely different issues, with each issue needing funding, must be stopped. Our journey will halt this process. Legislators vote for what issues they want to pass but are forced to accept many other issues full of pork. With voter input, the representatives would be more fearful of losing their jobs. Many of the massive bills so the voters can easily read and understand what is in that legislation. If we were informed and provided our input on pending legislation, we would know which representatives are staying prudent to their oath. Our journey working together with our input will provide our opinions and concerns to members of Congress before members of each house vote. With today's electronic surveys and polls, they can be completed easily, accurately, and quickly. With good questions, the information from the voters would be a valuable, timely resource to the representatives.

The American Rescue Plan Act also called the Covid – 19 stimulus Package which was passed by Congress was promoted as helping Americans suffering from the pandemic get past the terrible financial burden on individuals and businesses. So why is $519 billion going to bail out municipalities? USA Today, (usa-today.com), March 3, 2021, Titled Fact Check: Breaking down spending in the COVID – 19 relief bill. The problem is that 80 percent of the $1.9 trillion is not going to those who need help. That money is going to fund other entities that have nothing to do with the pandemic relief bill. More pork, pork, pork.

There are huge amounts of money to bail out those municipalities that have financially irresponsible governments. Those who made bad decisions and wasted their budget on items they couldn't afford should be responsible for their financial mismanagement. How is this fair to the municipalities who have done their job of fiscal responsibility? Another concern voters have is, if the municipalities have been financially mismanaged, what changes must be made once they get the money? If they fail to become fiscally responsible or elect new, ineffective leaders, the same mismanagement behavior will continue. How soon will it be before they need taxpayers to bail them out again?

Our journey will guide the voters in stopping the wasteful spending. Most people feel that this political divide will continue forever. This journey, new process, and new organization can close the divide and return us to the path the voters want America on.

I am confident there are millions of Americans who are logical, fair-minded, practical, and flexible in their thinking. Those individuals are reasonable and want to know the whole truthful story about what is going on in Washington. We need mature, motivated, and engaged people with common sense who will find this journey worthwhile. They want their voices heard. They want change! They will be excited to be part of the *Vote with Power* movement.

From now on, the voters will not just vote but stay informed and share their opinions. We will be fair-minded and responsible to stay in line with our Constitution and Bill of Rights. We will strive for equal treatment and opportunity for all Americans. We will stay assertive on urging our representatives to build an America that is in first place and stands for life, liberty, and the pursuit of happiness.

In the future, if the Constitution or Bill of Rights is not working for America, we need to make changes, but that doesn't mean we stop following our forefathers' foundational work. A simple resolve could be, when and if the Constitution begins to fail us, we will work to legally change the parts that no longer work for us. It would be strange if our society finds parts of our Constitution or amendments that are no longer working, those parts that are not in the best interests of the majority of our citizens. If that ever happens, we need to take the time and deeply research, discuss, and have the voters approve changes. But we must never violate what we have in place and have agreed on.

This journey is not about politics, it is about changing the process and level of representation. It is about unity and working together. We need to take a position and all work to alter the dysfunctional government and bring back our democracy. We need to vote in all elections. We need to stay informed and render our opinions through polls and other systems that will be set up during this journey.

We voters need to wake up and do our part. The major American wake-up calls have been the civil rights movement, Sputnik, 9/11, and COVID-19. This restructuring of who our representatives represent is a wake-up call to return the power to the voters. We need to take back our democracy! We are currently bystanders.

Our journey will hit a critical mass and gain success as soon as enough voices are heard. When enough voters commit and get involved, voter members will get information they need about what Congress is doing or not doing, and why. This will take place as soon as the voters are heard, answered, informed, respected, and represented. This will alter the way our government represents us. We just need enough voices.

Revenue and appropriation bills can only start in the House of Representatives. Any member or group of members of Congress can bring a bill to their chamber. Any member of Congress can initiate a bill based on their own insight and beliefs, or from the influence of any group or person.

We need to have all legislation provide a synopsis filled out on a transparency form so we the people can easily understand the source, magnitude, purpose, short- and long-term costs, who benefits, and who—if anyone—might be harmed. We need to know whether there are better alternatives, and whether this falls within the guidelines of the budget and the Constitution of the United States.

Both houses must pass a bill before the bill can go to the president for approval.

Legal bribery through unlimited campaign PACs and gerrymandering currently stack the political deck. This gives unfair party benefits in either passing or thwarting legislation. New regulations with transparency requirements and oversight will change these situations.

Once introduced, the bill is sent to the appropriate committee where members will debate and often redraft it. During this process, many congressional staff members play a critical role. My question is: How many representatives stay close enough to the bill to know what is in it as it changes?

During this stage we need to establish a new communication loop, so Congress does not get only the opinions and influence from big business, political parties, and money-strong special interests. This is where the voters need to have a communication method to provide their input and make it heard. This will create more equal representation and make sure our representatives know where the majority of their constituents stand.

Bills, after clearing the committee, get put on the docket in the House or Senate where the bill originated. At that time, all members of that house will debate it. More amendments and changes are made until eventually it comes to a vote.

At this stage there should be an added step. A neutral agency should check to ensure the legislation falls within the budget and is constitutional. It is also important that the cost and expense factors are agreed upon by both parties and there is no more "fuzzy math." This creates lack of transparency. We voters frequently hear two figures on what that bill will cost, often millions of dollars apart. The predictions and forecasts need to be agreed upon, and the research assessment from the CBO should come into play at this time. This will be a complex, difficult analysis. The figures need to be accurate. The only way to accomplish this is by having both parties agree on the presumptions and projections going into the research. All cost analyses must be completed by using the same assumptions. Otherwise, there will be a discrepancy in the results. That is a problem today.

Before voting on a bill, we need to have all members of Congress pledge they have read the bill and fully understand the impact it will have on the people. A sign-off form could easily provide this check. This is not political it is good business!

Bills, when passed, go to the other chamber, and go through changes and amendments again. The bill will go back and forth with ongoing amendments and changes until both houses pass identical versions of the bill. Once passed by both houses, it goes to the President for his/her approval or veto.

During this stage of the process, every bill needs to be researched to make sure it defines who will be responsible when the bill passes. That duty is to make sure the bill is properly implemented and tracked for results. In addition, we need to make sure the laws can realistically be implemented. Therefore, we need someone who is responsible for the follow-through and hold them accountable for reaching the goals and purposes of the bill. The stimulus bill passed, and a Warning came from an article in the ABC News that Experts warn of big fraud potential. I was later written in the business insider that as much as 50% of the stimulus unemployment money may have been stolen, Axios reports. This article was written on June 10, 2021, by Ayelet Sheffey (businessinsider.com) Doesn't this follow my position that indicates governments lack of responsibility and follow through.

We can get these changes made in the legislative process. From there we will get back to American's freedom and democracy. It will give the power back to the people to have a government of the people, by the people, and for the people. This journey will be the catalyst to take us there.

If we wait, we will be deeper in politics, deeper in debt, deeper in numbers of people in poverty, deeper in big city murders and crime, deeper in cultural splits, deeper in cancel culture, and deeper in the loss of our voter power. From there we will lose voters. We can sit back and give up or join this journey and change our representation.

We need to act now and put the voter pressure on our representatives to do what is right and in the best interests of their constituents, not the money or their political party alignment. The votes will eventually win over big money.

The more I listen to Americans talking about politics, the more I see they can be plotted on a political continuum. If you draw a horizontal line, you can place Americans in categories. First, mark the middle of the line where the centrists are positioned. Our government is currently void of centrists. We need new representatives that are of that mindset. As you move to the right, you find the Republican side, and on the left is the Democratic side.

The gridlock comes into play because of the extremist points of view. Those people are at the ends of the continuum. If you make a vertical mark either right or left of center, about 25 percent from the middle, you get the "somewhat party-aligned people." Changing politics will take groups of like-minded people who think America should always come first before politics. They need to be flexible and want more details on issues before taking a position. Votes across party lines are not highly emotional and not completely locked into their parties. They are tired of ever-present politics on all issues, and they are willing to accept common ground on issues.

When you make another vertical mark another 25 percent to either the right or the left from the middle, you get the "more intense about staying party-aligned." Those people are more emotional and less flexible on political issues. They will vote mostly along party lines. Those who are not locked into their party will want more information about the issues before making a judgment. They see the need for common ground and not grid-lock, and they want progress in America. They are slightly skeptical about the political information from either party. They do not often talk about politics.

If we make the last two vertical lines near the ends of the political continuum, we get the extreme party-aligned people. They are emotional, talk about politics frequently, often bash the other party, do not listen to logic, or have a need for more details. They believe their party is right, and they would rather have gridlock than give in. They feel politics is a win-or-lose proposition. They vote 100 percent for their party candidates. They are often blinded by their party's information.

The more people and representatives who position themselves near the ends of the continuum, the less positive progress our government can deliver. They are more radical when thinking about our government's purpose and success. We cannot allow these few to steer our policies, values, and lifestyles. We need more independent thinkers who are willing to move away from party lines. We need those independents to step up, get informed, vote, and stay involved to keep America a progressive democracy.

We need to keep track of voting records, by state, or how each of our representatives voted. Is it along party lines most of the time? Does their voting record show their interest is in helping big business, big banks, lobbyists, and wealthy individuals, or is it for the best interests of the American people?

This will take time and not be easy to accomplish. Our representatives are comfortable operating in a vacuum within their party groups, plus being entertained and influenced by lobbyists.

Since you have read this book to this point, I hope you are interested in taking this journey. Your help is needed to make sure we are successful. We cannot be stopped by cancel culture, setback, threats, or diversions. This will work once we have the representatives' attention and get them to see value in what we are offering. This will threaten their existence and their comfort in the way they have been approaching their jobs for years. We will persist until they hear us, answer our questions, respect us, inform us, and represent us. If they keep fighting this change, they will live under the threat of losing our votes and their jobs.

When we see the bills before they are passed, and we find pork, we need to immediately have the politicians explain and justify why they are voting the way they are. At first, they will not want to take the time to give us true, full answers. This must change.

Some politicians will think this journey will remove their power and influence. They will need to be educated on the real benefits to them. For those who are afraid of the voters having too much control, they need to review their oath of office and compare it with who they are currently representing. The voters are the ones who they have the duty to represent.

This journey will make the jobs of congressional members easier. They will first have to accept and adapt to the new processes. Our new two-way open, honest disclosure process will become a system they like. This journey and organization will provide a means for knowing what their constituents think and want. This will open dialogue where Congress and the voters can truly see each other's point of view and purpose. Congress will have a much better understanding of what voters want. The voters will have more input and a better understanding of why their representatives vote the way they do. This means our representatives will represent those they are supposed to be representing. It will lower the representatives' stress level from passing bills and laws that are against the will of their own district voters. Currently, most of their voting is on behalf of big money influencers or their party. By signing their oath of office through the ethics of the office, our representatives should not fail to represent their constituents. The unethical representatives must feel pressure when they misrepresent staying within the oath of office, they took. Our representatives often break their oaths and act in unethical ways by failing to vote in the best interests of their constituents.

The advocated state communications loop centers, explained in this book, will be funded by small monthly membership fees—no dollars from any foreign entities, big business, big banks, big tech companies, or political parties.

This is a plan of action. We cannot afford to read about this idea and then turn away from implementing it. Now is the time we stopped letting our government tell us what is good for us and move forward on their agenda, not ours. The purpose for our journey is to turn this written plan into an action road map for activating change.

The last responsibility is to make sure all voters get the facts on each incumbent so they can make a choice in the best interests of the people of their state to either reelect or vote them out!

For us as individuals and families, we need to look at government and the major issues differently. We are the bosses and leaders.

This journey will not work for those people who want our government to do everything for them. If you decide not to take this journey, you will be giving up freedom of choice. Many countries around the world have Communist parties, dictators, and oligarchies that give their people few choices. They lack freedom and opportunity. We cannot go there. Look at the direction our Congress is taking us, near the plateau of a different kind of governance, one we do not want. We must stand up and act.

This journey is also to correct the lack of investigation into and removing the power from the big money players. Bank of America spied on their customers. The bank used the account activities of customers who were in Washington DC at the time of the Capitol building invasion. They used credit card spending to indicate what they bought, where they bought and when. This information was shared with the Justice Department without telling their customers. This was also supposedly without any request from our enforcement system. This needs to be researched to determine if what they did was legal. It does not sound legal. If it is not, we the voters have the right to the hear the entire story. If it is illegal, what will our judicial system do about it? Even if it was legal, what happened to privacy?

These were not criminals; they were just in the wrong place at the wrong time. Some were brought into police stations and questioned because of something they bought or paid for, which they had the freedom to do.

Another recent win for us being represented and treated fairly came from the California court that stopped the attorney general from using his own standard of justice instead of the justice for all documents. California has a three-strike rule for punishing criminals. The more crimes you commit, the tougher the sentencing becomes. The attorney general decided that he would not abide by this law and use minimal punishment or no punishment for criminals who were caught with multiple crimes.

Another part of our journey will be to redirect the emphasis of some of our programs. For instance, we need fresh, workable, implementable ideas for solving the low-income problems in many parts of our country. The people living there need help. Not handouts but real help. How often does Congress or a committee ever come up with reasonable, great ideas for fixing major problems? This journey will help develop new programs and those that are already working to help underserved and low-income people. They will get better education, better health care, and safe neighborhoods, and renew their culture values and build better family structures. This will take motivation, creativity, and new concepts to the citizens with needs to get them excited to take advantage of new programs. They will need to be involved in the planning and committed to getting their neighbors involved. As many citizens as we can recruit will need to understand and take on the responsibility of changing the communication process of our political system. This is needed to provide the opportunities to become what we want and live the lifestyle we hope for. It is also needed to unite us to work together to give the same opportunities to all Americans It will take money. Where can we get it? Let us take some of the billions of dollars we spend in foreign countries and use it to help develop and improve opportunities for our own citizens.

Our journey will stop the name-calling and blaming. What values do those have? We must ask those who name-call what they have done financially, using their time and energy to actually help those in need. I would bet most of the name-callers have not invested anything in being part of the solution.

Chapter 17

The New Voter and Representative Cooperative Approach

To make the changes advocated in this book, we need a new style government, one where our representatives are willing to work with their constituents. We must use a communication and operational system that is well thought out, a government where voters and representatives are motivated to work with each other.

We must have a format that changes the way we now interact. No more name-calling, blaming, or doing nothing. No more wasteful spending into bankruptcy, not hearing, answering, respecting, informing, or representing the voters.

This best and most efficient process will build in ways to interact in a practical manner due to the large numbers of voters. Once the communication loop centers are operating and we have polls, surveys, questionnaires, and focus groups, we will be ready. These information-gathering tools will be written by professional researchers. We need the data to be accurate, timely, and reliable. The forms need to be easy for the voters to fill out in a short amount of time. When the input from the needed number of voters based on statistical representation is available, great progress will take place.

Huge corporations' CEOs are worth billions of dollars and donate millions to campaigns. Therefore, they get things done their way. There is good news. We voters must remember that the CEO only has the same voting power as you and me. So, we need to de-power the money by following this journey and have the voter masses direct our wishes upon our representatives. If our representatives fight against this new system, they will receive poor performance reviews. The performance reviews will track voting records. This will include the percent of time they voted, percent of time they voted as their constituents wanted, how many times they voted on behalf of their party or others, how they have stayed in touch with their constituents, and the quality and timeliness of information desired and shared with their voters.

If our representatives get bad grades on their performance reviews and fail to improve, they will need to be voted out at their next election.

I am not advocating that we tell the representatives how to vote or think, but they will have good input from their constituents to make better decisions, which represent the wishes of their constituents. In case anyone forgot, this is their job.

This proposal will work, but only if many voters will get and stay involved. By getting reliable information, giving their opinions, answering questions, and taking part in polling, surveys, and focus groups, their voices will be heard.

There is good news for the voters who fear retribution from taking part in this journey. They will be kept anonymous as they will be members of a private voter group. This will turn the direction of America as we become united. We will once again have Congress working with and for us.

We need to alter our legislators' mindsets to one of "let the voters help us make decisions."

A new calmness, sharing, understanding, dialogue, and non-judgmental attitude will become the usual tone. This new process through two-way communication will bring about common ground. Both voters and representatives will have a way to understand and appreciate each other's desires, needs, and challenges. This will provide consistency and will correct the current dysfunctional communication system.

Here is my assessment of what we need to do and what I am willing to provide. We need the power and a reason for our representatives to join our journey. That reason will be loss of their jobs.

We must have a way for our representatives to get our input consistently, frequently, and in timely order to keep them well-informed of their constituents' point of view.

The state communication loop offices will be the center to conduit dialogue between the voters in that state and their representatives and create a dual system of transparency and accountability.

These centers will not be political, judgmental, or have an agenda of their own. They will represent all voters: liberals, conservatives, independents, Republicans, Democrats, and all others. Their job is to gather voter information and pass it on to the representatives. The new government will need voters who are committed and take on the responsibility to work through the centers to keep our representatives informed, in addition to gathering information from their representatives and passing it on to the voters. This is how any responsible organization functions. They need to review their employees' and staff's progress and performance.

Voting records kept by the centers will help voters make their own independent voting decisions on candidates. These reports will point out the level of influence voters have. It will be a running report of the way the representatives voted. They will also track the level of involvement in Congress and their leadership and management efforts and results. The centers will also record any spending votes that are over budget and/or pork spending. This will be the new system representatives will be rated on. This will help voters make informed decisions on who to vote for in the next election. This is the only way to check the representatives' progress and how they have represented their constituents. This will allow representatives access, through the centers, for getting input from thousands of their voters by only communicating with the center director. They will have results from their constituents through polls, surveys, questionnaires, focus groups, and other research results.

No longer will members of Congress only have access to the opinions and input from only a few voters, forcing them to assume the input from those few represents all the voters in their district. The new system I'm advocating will allow for representatives to perform their jobs by representing their voters on a more accurate level. They will have true and almost total information along with the knowledge of what their voters want.

This information source is not more restrictive or a policing system. Our legislators, at first, will fear that this is an attempt to hover over them. The real purpose is to change the frequency and tone of the communication. The centers will be a new place to gather information for both voters and representatives. It will clarify many opinions and weaken the use of slanted judgment and Congress operating from the wrong pressure points.

Most of the time the voters find out what is in those bills and laws after they have been passed, after the changes have been made. At that time, the normal voter response is, "Whose stupid idea was that? Why did they do that? What were they thinking? Why are they wasting our money?"

This new communication system will help our representatives in Congress better serve their voters and improve their ratings and their image. This will provide the good representatives job security. This dialogue will also help with voters' ideas that are never heard or thought of by anyone in Congress.

This is the only way that voters can get and stay involved without investing huge amounts of money or time, which our system of representation was designed to avoid.

Each center will offer voters memberships that will cost less than 28 cents per day for founding members. Is America and your future worth it? You decide. In return, the members will be kept up to date on what their representatives are working on and their voting record.

They will receive emails once per week to keep them current. They also will have the opportunity to call or email their centers with questions, concerns, ideas, and to get information. When the voter information and questions are on an important level, they will be passed from the director to the appropriate legislators. The voters will also be kept in the loop of the performance reviews of the members of Congress. This system is how Congress will be held accountable and required to be transparent. They will also be involved with the polls and research the center will be providing on critical issues for Congress and the voters. Eventually trust, honesty, and openness will be gained on both sides.

There is another huge benefit to the members of Congress. This journey and organization will take some of the pressure off handling the many letters, emails, and phone calls they get from their constituents. Many of those contacts are created due to lack of information. It will also help with lowering the number of complaints. When people are involved and know what is going on and feel involved, they will feel better and have less complaints. Many of our representatives do not have the time, so they fail to respond to their constituents' requests in a timely manner, which makes the voters feel they do not care.

The centers will be funded by the membership fees. The fees will fund the searching and hiring the best director and staff members which can be found. Their tasks are to keep the polling, research, effective two-way communication, and to promote the center for new members.

The "vote with power" centers will be set up as information and distribution centers under the guidance of the national headquarters. The purpose of the national headquarters is to handle concerns and issues that are too cumbersome for the state offices to oversee and for issues that are beyond the authority or magnitude of the state level office.

The "vote with power" headquarters will also be involved with national issues and marketing methods to promote voter member growth.

The journey's national headquarters and the state offices will be structured as for-profit organizations. This is representative of my beliefs and passion for capitalism. Capitalism creates the economic success of America. Nonprofit organizations have their place, and most do wonderful work. I want this to be an independently funded organization of the people.

This journey creates hope and will work. However, to experience it, we must get all voters involved and take action to live in the America of hope, safety, prosperity, fairness, and opportunity for all.

Chapter 18

Why We Need to Stop the Pork Spending

We have a national debt load of close to $28 trillion as seen on the national debt load clock. (usdebtclock.org). This is in catastrophic proportions. We owe foreign countries over $7 trillion, much of it to China and Japan.

How safe does that make you feel? If you want to have a stomachache, go to *usdebtclock.org* and see how our interest due and national debt figures grow faster than you can read the numbers.

To put our debt in perspective, if every taxpayer in our country wrote a check for $222,191 today, we could pay off the debt. Is that amount in your checkbook? Would you rather keep our government's tab growing and have your children and grandchildren pay way more in a few years?

Should we just let China and Japan take over our assets and own us? Do you want to help stop the bleeding? We need to change the mindset and open-spending approach used by our representatives. We need to stop the overspending, live within a budget, and start paying off our debt.

Most of the spending goes to five areas: Medicare/Medicaid, Social Security, defense/war, and interest on the debt. If we reduce and eventually pay off the debt, that interest payment money would build the reserve funds for those other programs. We could stop worrying about where the money will come from to keep these programs healthy.

There are more than 157 million Americans in our workforce. According to the Pew Research article "10 facts about American workers. Written by Drew Desilver August 29, 2019. (pewresearch.org). We have a US population of approximately 330 million. Due to the aging of our population, there is no reason to anticipate a much high number joining our workforce, unless our borders stay open, and immigration continues at a fast pace. The extra costs due to the aging of our citizens going on retirement funding, along with their increasing longevity, is the cause of these critical programs being underfunded now.

Official U.S. Census Bureau statistics estimate that 40 million persons are living in poor economic position or poverty. (aspe.hhs.gov/poverty-estim) We must stop overspending our budget, borrowing to spend, and printing money, to help fund America's other critical needs. We need new programs to get the inner city, minority, and poverty-stricken people out of their trapped lives. They need hope, education, effective life skills mentoring, training, and cultural values to learn responsibility and build their families.

The financial goal for our new journey is to get the voters engaged and consistently focused on what the politicians are spending our money on. If constituents really knew the truth of where their kids' and grandkids' money is going, changes would be made. Once the voters fully understand the magnitude of the spending and what it is spent on, there would be and should be a revolt.

There is no longer any justification for trading pork for pork. If we have a single-issue bill to deal with and understand the merits and trade-offs, we can force common sense within budget spending.

We are close to bankruptcy now! Congress does not want to face our situation or do anything about it. We must stop printing and borrowing money. We also need to stop spending more than we take in. If you owned a business and spent more than your revenue, your business would fail, and you would be out of business.

We need to look at our national government and run the finances as if it were a successful business, which it should be! The same questions should be asking of our representative when they are overspending the budget. What exactly is the plan for using the money? Why did they need the money? Who will oversee the funds distribution for efficiency and to ensure there are no leaks? Who will be accountable for getting the expected results from this expenditure? How do we guard against wasting any of these funds? I would bet that if you got in touch with your representatives, they could not answer any of those questions. They always vote to spend money without detailed goals, defined purposes, well-developed plans, and tracking tools. It is easy to spend other people's money when you are not held responsible for the outcome.

Our government spends money like a flowing river. It just keeps rolling along. We need new regulations on how any money is spent. Often our current allocated funds are sucked up in the administration of those funds.

I also advocated to get our representatives to stop using pork trade for negotiating. Congress used pork trading to hold the other party hostage. This spending only helps a few people or big business. Most of the money has nothing to do with the advancement and rights of we the common people.

In your business, what would happen if you spent a lot of money on anything that did not advance your sales or profitability? Your cash flow would suffer, and your company would go broke.

Money should not be used as a negotiating tool. If the bill does not stand on its own merits, we cannot afford it. Therefore, like your family finances, we do not need it! You have to live without it. Or you could charge it and pay for it many times over.

We need to stop spending money we do not have. We often give countries financial and other costly aid. This is based on the assumption that other countries will like and respect us. We have also been told the money will promote democracy. It has never worked and will not ever work. Most countries we give money to hate us. How about Pakistan, who not only hates us but hides dangerous terrorists we are looking for? Every year we give a gift of billions of dollars to Pakistan. We need to track what we get in return.

Countries, like people, only respect you if you respect yourself and strongly follow your core values. We have a horrendous amount of national debt, and it is getting worse minute by minute. One of our core values must be to spend money wisely.

In reality, we need to be concerned about the money we owe China and Japan. When will the loans be called? How much power do they have over us? When will they own us? You know what the banks do when they call your mortgage loan. They own your assets.

Using pork as a negotiating tool has caused our government huge problems because the process of trading pork is so ingrained in the way legislators get votes for their proposals. Unless we the voters speak up, this process will continue forever.

Pork spending is also eroding opportunities and future economic success, especially for our children and grandchildren. What will their lives look like if they have to pay a large percentage of their income to interest paid on debt?

We have spent trillions of dollars fighting wars in other countries. The purpose was to help them survive. We hear those wars are to keep us safe. Do we have any proof that this really works? The cost in dollars, injured warriors and even those who died protecting us must be justified. Thank you to our honored heroes for your sacrifice. Our duty is to do what is fair and needed for all our first responders and military personnel.

Many of those countries have assets such as oil and other resources. Other countries who use us to fight their wars should be paying us. But we just spend the money, and even worse, we lose and ruin American lives.

Since those with the money are in control, they are protected and hide behind our congressional leaders.

Since those with the money are in control, they are protected and hide behind our congressional leaders.

How successful are businesses that hide information from their owners? Remember, when you voted, you hired a representative for the purpose of reaching your goals and protecting your lifestyle and liberty. You did not vote for them to work against you. Part of the deal was not to give our representatives an open checkbook.

If you own a business, can you afford to spend billions on products, services, and assets that give little or no return on your investments? Of course not.

In your business, either you or someone else must have the knowledge and skills in financial management. In a financially healthy business, you need the right people, who have the ability, authority, and responsibility to make good financial decisions and control the money, to keep the business financially sound.

If we gave members of Congress a financial management test, how many could pass it? Do those who could pass it fail to stand up for good financial controls? How many just do not care?

We must stop spending money on special interest organizations or projects. Once the voters get involved, we can slow the unrealistic and wasteful spending. The voters from each state will let their representative know what they would like approved and not approved. We need to know why our representative too often follow their own opinions—another cooperative unifying thought. Even if a group of citizens from one state think the spending has merits, there is another consideration. All Americans need to assess the true impact on the general public for investing our money in these projects. Is this spending request really going to help us as a country or most Americans? There is an important option to spending our tax dollars. This alternative should be used in case a project or item is important to a small or medium-size group of people. The cause does not have the interest of all or most of the citizens of America, not enough interest to have the money come from our federal budget. Those groups who are interested could proceed by getting volunteers and donations enough to pay for and implement the project, rather than fund their pet project from our national budget. Often funding pet projects serves as repayment, as a thank-you to campaign donors. This alternative is used all the time but must be expanded to use our federal taxes to benefit the majority. It is great for individuals who have a passion for a program. They keep their independence and leave the tax dollars for the major concerns of all voters.

Chapter 19

Conclusion

Most Americans are fed up with the politics. We need to become less political.

Yesterday I was talking with a friend, and the discussion turned to politics, as it often does with him. He addressed our current government's dysfunction with frustration, anger, and lack of hope.

He mentioned that he does not watch the news and hates the political stalemates and finger-pointing. He does not like the direction our country is going. Not knowing what he can do, he stated emphatically that he is just giving up.

According to a September 14, 2020, Gallup Poll, only 20% of U.S. adults say they trust the government in Washington DC to "do the right thing" just about always. This means that almost all Americans feel the same about our government.

My concern is that most Americans will take the easy way out. They will hide from the challenge of turning our government around. Sadly, most Americans want to stay in their own environment and not get involved in the bigger picture. The question is: Are they happy with our government as it is? They should also note, if left alone, our government and lifestyles will only get worse.

There is hope. There is a plan. The voters can take back the reins with the power to guide our representatives and steer our country in the right direction.

The journey I have explained tells what must be done and how we can get it done.

This approach is to fix the operating processes and the way Congress functions. This plan will be fair and helpful to all Republicans, Democrats, Tea Partiers, liberals, or conservatives. They can maintain their philosophies, values, and beliefs. Our journey plan is to make functional changes. We can find common ground and all live within our core values.

By changing our broken system, we will get voters back in the communication loop and force our representatives to be more transparent, and more accountable. They will hear us, inform us, answer us, respect us, and represent us.

Please, do not give up. Your help is needed badly. We need to change our government processes and our level of representation. This is a serious issue if you care about your family's future and the future of all Americans! When we start voting with power, our lives will change.

Together we can fix our government!

When considering America's future, the two prevailing questions on most people's minds are: *Is it too late?* And *If not, what can be done?*

Now is the time to get answers to these two questions. We will be faced with another election in a few months from the time this book was written, many people will not know who to vote for. For the voters who know who they will choose, it is not a representative but a party. They are locked into always voting for whatever their party wants. We need to vote for the best candidates, not always for a party. Most voters feel they are no longer voting for a representative but for a party. We will never get some party-addicted voters to see the light. They are giving up their independence and freedom. To be true Americans, all voters need to do their duty to vote and then stay engaged in directing their representatives to improve the lives of all citizens, not always following their party. No matter what the issue is, they will also want their representatives to vote following party wishes.

The complaint is that both parties have become too extreme in their positioning and actions. The constant political bickering and blaming the other party has become the normal mode of operation. This has caused major function breakdowns and loss of progress in both houses of Congress.

We are dangerously close to our government taking away our progress, opportunities, our freedom, and our democracy. Our country is about to fail! We need get off the slippery slope to oligarchy.

To get back to democracy and put the power back in the hands of the voters, we need to:

1. Have our votes count more than the wishes of money contributors.
2. Create a communication loop between the constituents and our representatives, giving us understanding and influence over their political party.
3. Get Congress to listen to our ideas and opinions more than the media and poll results.
4. Change the operational system of Congress to change the way they function. Both political parties are dysfunctional and need our help as outsiders to promote

the change. We the voters need to take a position of being the insiders.

5. Dilute the overbearing politics affecting almost every aspect of our lives. We need more oversight by having our representatives in Congress become more transparent, open, and honest in their communications. Representation of constituents should be their top priority.

6. We need to get the new centers to provide the voters with representative voting records and performance reviews.

7. Get Congress to put the interest of we the voters first: hear us, answer us, inform us, respect us, and represent us.

8. We need to develop a system for proper candidate screening.

To enact these changes, voters will need to get the attention of the incumbents in Congress who are intent on winning their next election. Those in office who will take our lead in these changes will help this journey succeed. In addition, it is also a great time to get the attention of those who will be running for office for the first time. We must set up criteria for qualifying candidates for office and make sure they are committed to representing us. After we have their attention, we must then create enough pressure to cause them to desire the change to benefit their constituents, for the good of our country. Last, we must follow through so the right actions are taken to reform the political parties and end big money control over our political system government and country.

You have a choice; do nothing and live in an America you won't like or help unite with thousands of others to change our dysfunctional government by joining our journey!

Visit www.votewithpower.com to join our movement.

If you need further convincing, here are the reasons most voters will want to get involved:

They are you tired of Congress begging for your vote but then representing their party, big money, and power grabs before they do their job by representing you? We need to change those priorities.

If you are worried about your children's and grandchildren's futures of good financial health and job opportunities, you need to get involved to stop the pork over-the-budget spending by Congress.

We must also keep taxes in line with our budget and desires and yet pay for Medicare, Medicaid, and Social Security. These needed programs will only work and be sustained if they are managed by plans and best practices in the same manner as a successful business, not the government's current practice of kicking the can of financial responsibility down the road.

The answer to correcting current congressional behavior is to get and stay involved. Ask questions, give feedback, and lead our representatives in staying within their oath.

Do you agree that we must change the following?

No more rogue, party-driven voting or representing any entity besides we the voters.

We must build cooperation and trust by identifying and reminding Congress that they work for us.

Represent the American people or get out!

Make America first or get out!

Vote to stay within the budget or get out!

Stop trading pork for votes or get out!

Put together and stay with a plan for eliminating our debt or get out!

Cooperate with the transparency and accountability centers or get out!

Stop voting mostly along party lines or get out!

If we, the voters, stick our heads in the sand, as we have done for years, our legacy will be one of helping others take our freedoms, opportunities, safety, family success, peace, happiness, and liberty. Do you want that for your epitaph? Your freedom is only protected by the influence we the voters have over our representatives. This is the only way to keep our democracy alive. The only way to keep our influence is through Vote With Power.

About the Author

Dennis Bowersox holds a bachelor's degree in sociology with a minor in psychology and education from Western Michigan University, and a master's degree in counseling from Central Michigan University. He has taught psychology, business, and leadership and acted in the capacity of a change agent while consulting with many companies on organizational systems development. He is a published author, with his first book in 2007, *Financial Intervention, Creating Money for Life.* His second book came out in 2012, *Our Government is Killing Us! An Invitation to Help Fix Our Government and Cure Our Economy.* He has purchased one franchise and started six profitable businesses. Denny is a lifelong learner of history, government, small business, and economics. He is inspired to have American voters join his movement in changing the way voters are represented in Congress. His journey with voters will take back the power of influence over political parties, big money, and big tech companies. He wants to share his journey and organizational system to get our government on the right path, which will create a bright future for all Americans.

CPSIA information can be obtained
at www.ICGtesting.com
Printed in the USA
LVHW010250230821
695875LV00008B/243